Freedom—
Not License!

A. S. Neill

HART PUBLISHING COMPANY, INC. • NEW YORK CITY

Contents

WHAT THIS BOOK IS ABOUT   7

FREEDOM—NOT LICENSE!   11
    Self-Regulation   21

ANTI-LIFE ATTITUDES   27
    Manners   27
    Duty and Responsibility   30
    Respect   36
    Conventionalism   38
    Dishonesty   39
    Discrimination   41

SCHOOL   45
    Homework   60

SEX   63
    Sex Education   63
    Masturbation   64
    Nudity   65
    Masculinity and Femininity   66
    Menstruation   67
    Circumcision   67
    Contraceptives   68
    Homosexuality   71

INFLUENCING CHILDREN   75
    Career   78
    Censorship   81
    Undesirable Companions   83
    Religion   84
    Character Molding   88
    Marriage   94

PROBLEMS OF CHILDHOOD   99
    Spanking   99
    Destructiveness   102
    Bullying and Fighting   105
    Lying   108
    Stealing   112
    Sulking   115
    Television   115
    Food and Eating   117
    Thumb-Sucking   119
    Sleep   119
    Toys   121
    Fantasy   123

PROBLEMS OF ADOLESCENCE   125
    Staying Out Late   125
    Cursing   130
    Driving a Car   134
    Smoking   135
    Drinking   138
    Drug Addiction   140
    Make-Up   143
    Clothes   145
    Money   147

Restrictions   150
Defiance   150
Intermarriage   154

FAMILY TENSION   155
    Parental Disagreement   155
    Grandparents   162
    Broken Home   162
    Sibling Rivalry   163
    Adoption   167
    Parental Attitude   169

THERAPY   171
    Fear   171
    Stuttering   173
    Psychotherapy   173
    Introversion   181

A FINAL WORD   183

INDEX   188

He drew a circle that shut me out—
Heretic, rebel, a thing to flout.
But Love and I had the wit to win:
We drew a circle that took him in!

EDWIN MARKHAM

What This Book Is About

How can one distinguish between freedom and license? My publisher in the U. S. A. implores me to write a whole book in explanation of these terms, saying, "You must, for so many American parents who have read SUMMERHILL feel guilty about the strict way they have treated their child, and then tell their child that from now on he is free. The result is usually a spoiled brat, for the parents have scant notion of what freedom is. They do not realize that freedom is a give and take—*freedom for parents* as well as freedom for the child. As I understand it, freedom does not mean that the child can do everything he wants to do, nor have everything he wants to have."

Yes, that simply stated, is the crux of the matter. Freedom, over-extended, turns into license.

I define license as interfering with another's freedom. For example, in my school a child is free to go to lessons or stay away from lessons because that is his own affair, but he is not free to play a trumpet when others want to study or sleep.

When I was in America, I would have an occasion, now and then, to visit a professor or a doctor. When I arrived his wife and children might be in the room. The children remained and monopolized the conversation.

When an American visitor came to visit me at Summerhill today, three children were in my room. "Come on, kids." I said, "buzz off. I want to talk to this visitor." And off they went without a murmur.

Of course, the principle would have applied the other

7

way around, too. My pupils have often told me to clear out
when they wanted privacy—when rehearsing a play, for
example.

Every child is selfish—Me first! Parents must appreciate and accept that stage for what it is; at the same time,
they must refuse to give Junior the license to do everything he wants to do.

A proper answer is *"Yes, Bobby, you may use my car
tools to fix your bike, but you have got to put the tools
back in the car trunk when you are finished with them."*
That answer may spell discipline to you—maybe it is discipline—but for me it is just life's give and take.

*How can children develop self-control if they are never
restrained from doing whatever they want to do?* is a question I am often asked.

But who ever advocated a child's always doing what
he wants to do? I certainly never did. Junior can decide
what he *doesn't* want to do. For example, study Latin. But
he is not free to choose to play cops and robbers in father's
car.

What is the true definition of self-control? Is it just
good manners, like curbing your profanities when you are
golfing with the Baptist minister? No, in my opinion self-
control means *the ability to think of other people,* to respect the rights of other people.

No self-controlled man ever sits down with others and
helps himself to half the salad in the salad bowl.

According to anecdote, Frank Harris once boasted that
he had dined at the best houses in London, "Yes, Frank,"
said Oscar Wilde, "once!"

In my book SUMMERHILL, I pointed out that "It is this
distinction between freedom and license that many parents

cannot grasp. In the disciplined home, the children have *no* rights. In the spoiled home, they have *all* the rights. The proper home is one in which children and adults have *equal* rights."

Since the publication of SUMMERHILL in 1960, I have received hundreds of letters from all over the world from parents and from children. Most of these letters have come from the United States. By and large, the questions revert to the fundamentals of freedom in the home. This book presents excerpts from some of these letters and the salient passages of my replies.

The reader will find that I have nothing to say now that is dramatically new. The principles upon which the Summerhill School is based, the fundamentals of my methods of handling children, have been stated by me in full in my book SUMMERHILL: *A Radical Approach to Child Rearing.* What one will find here is an extension of that philosophy— the application of Summerhill principles to the specific situations that constantly arise in the American home.

Freedom—Not License!

I am a new mother and my husband and I would like to raise our child in an atmosphere of freedom. But as we discuss this, we seem not at all to be sure where freedom ends and indulgence takes over, or even when to intervene as a matter of safety. For example, should we set up standards of cleanliness and of respect for property?

Safety is essential. You have to protect your child. You have to see that he does not play on busy roads or jump into deep water. Common sense in these matters is all that is required.

But it is not so easy to answer the question when safety is not a factor. Take cleanliness. Any mother knows that diapers must be washed, that children must be bathed, that good food must be provided. But cleanliness must not be made a fetish or it will lead to complexes. We over-exaggerate the importance of cleanliness. When I was a boy, I knew three farmers who, I am sure, never had a bath in their lives. They all lived to be over 90. Far too many children are over-washed because the neighbors might see a dirty face.

But the fact is that almost every child likes a hot bath. It is my observation that only a child who has been made defiant will balk at taking a bath.

How much should a young mother do in the way of demanding respect for property? Every infant has to learn the laws of mine and thine. If a child is reared properly, there should be little difficulty here. I can say to a child of five: "Come on, get out of my car; it's mine," and I get no hostile reaction. Even the youngest pupil knows that he cannot come into my garden and take away a barrow or a rake. Children soon accept these rules, that is if touching things or taking things is not made into an affair of rebuke or anger.

One cannot lay down laws about freedom and license; the boundary has to be judged by the individual parent. Often you have to say no to a small child, however much you believe in freedom. Houses are made for adults, and in the process of fitting into a home, the child has a thousand difficulties. *"Don't touch that vase!" "Stop pulling the cat's tail." "Don't scratch the grand piano with that nail."* To a child of three, a piano with its polished veneer is a lovely blackboard for chalk or a nice wall in which to drive nails— nothing more. The difficulty is how to preserve what we value in things, and at the same time let the child develop in his own way and time. Obviously, never to say no is to bring up a spoiled child who will be incapable of facing later realities. Such a kid will grow up to expect the world to provide everything he wants.

When it comes to freedom and license, there's no Bible, no encyclopedia to consult, no final authority. The onus is on every parent to use his head. All that can be postulated is that never must the child be made afraid or be made to feel guilty.

So much depends on your personality. If you are a fairly placid woman, if your love life with your husband is good, if you are sufficiently removed either geographically or psychically from interfering relations, then you have a chance, a *good* chance of rearing a child that will be as free as possible from neurosis. It will be up to you to make decisions every day about when to say yes and when to say no.

My Johnny troops his young pals into the living room after school. I object because they muss things up. Now and then, they leave peanut shells on the carpet. Nor are they too considerate of the furniture. I earnestly approve of Johnny having friends and I am very fond of his companions, but I would like to herd that young gang into Johnny's room. Johnny objects and says his room is too small for six young lads. He claims that this is his house, too, and that he should be allowed to have his friends occupy and enjoy the main room. Is this an argument for freedom or one for license? Johnny is 14.

It looks like the latter to me. Freedom is doing what you like so long as you do not interfere with the freedom of others. Johnny is interfering with your freedom.

The truth is that children should not be in the same environment as adults. Our bookcases, our ornaments, our wall clocks mean nothing to a child. But alas, only the rich can provide especially designed rooms for the child. Children should have their quarters built by the village blacksmith. Of course, the reality is that children do occupy the quarters used by adults for adult pursuits, and the reality is that adults, at times, do require quiet and do require aesthetic decoration.

In Summerhill, we don't allow pupils to enter the staffroom and strew it with peanuts and chewing gum wrappers. In my wife's sitting room, we insist that young visitors must behave themselves if they are invited to watch TV.

I'd say to Johnny: "Look here, my son, you can bring your pals in as often as you like, but if they drown the house in noise and throw things on the floor, out they go."

No one should rule a home; every member of a home

has an equal right to comfort and peace and quiet. To allow a boy to get all he wants is just turning him into a young tyrant.

My son of eight constantly interrupts my conversations with my wife. We don't want to sit on him and throttle his personality. What can we do about it?

Difficult to answer when I don't know what you are like as parents. Most likely you have allowed your boy more license than freedom, and are now reaping the whirlwind. Maybe his constant talking may be due to bottled up questions you did not answer earlier. Maybe he is just a born gasbag!

I don't know what relationship there is between you and your boy. He might be interrupting you because he wants to rile you. Or because his Oedipus makes him want to keep father from mother. How can one analyze a situation one hasn't seen?

I generally say to parents: Don't let your child boss you, if you don't boss him. Don't let your child interrupt you, if you don't interrupt him. Making little Junior into a kind of a statue on a pedestal is bad for him.

Many parents nowadays have some notion that by thwarting their child they will turn him into a moron or into an Al Capone. Nonsense! Parents should say no when a no is necessary. Parents dare not let their child browbeat them.

I was talking with an American business man. His son of 13 was bored by our conversation. He jumped up, interrupted, and cried, "Daddy, give me the car key. I'll take a ride." "Okay, son," said the father, and he handed the boy the key to his new Cadillac. That to me was just foolishness and license—not to mention the criminality of putting a death machine into the hands of a young.boy.

I repeat and repeat the words: "Freedom must come from both sides." The child must be free to talk without interruption, and the parent is to be free to talk without interruption. The child should be able to refuse interference by the parent with his personal life and his personal things, and the parent should be free to refuse his son his Cadillac, or his golf clubs, or his necktie, or the peace of his study room, or the interruption of his afternoon nap.

My boy is four. He yells, and screams, and makes a great deal of noise. Is he of an age when I can teach him that he should be mindful of the rights of others?

Yes, tell him to shut up, but do not clothe the protection in morality. To garnish with sermons is both wrong and futile.

Even a child of four will begin to grasp what the rights of others mean. In our weekly school parliament at Summerhill, a four- or five-year-old will begin to talk or make a noise. The chairman says: "Nellie, be quiet, this is a meeting." She is quiet—if it is only for five minutes. But she feels no fear because the chairman's voice is not one of stern authority. The children here are in an atmosphere in which they feel they are approved of—even when they are being a damned nuisance.

In a good home—one in which there is no fear—a child of four will not be harmed by being asked to keep quiet.

I am well aware that a girl of 15 has lots of friends, but my Jeannette is on the phone interminably. Our friends call us and can't break through the sound barrier. Should we allow Jeannette to talk as long as she wants to, or is she exercising license?

I guess she is. I'd simply say: "Look here, my girl, you aren't the only pebble on the beach. Others want to phone, so get off the line."

My daughter claims that she is bringing up her child in an atmosphere of freedom, but to me it seems she is being extremely permissive. The kids get just about everything they want, and are unmindful of the needs and wishes of adults. She seems to think she is following Summerhill precepts. I am not so sure. What comment can you offer?

It is not easy to comment for I don't know the situation. Recently, I said to the mother of one of my young pupils: "Why do you fly off the handle when your boy uses a swear word or breaks a cup?"

Her answer: "I am not a happy woman. My husband has not slept with me for five years. My life is one long frustration, and it gets on my nerves and I shout at the kids."

Giving children everything they want can mean that they are getting substitutes for the love the parents cannot give them. In a good home, the children are not allowed to rule the roost; they, like the adults, are partners in a busy, happy going concern.

On the other hand, you may be the wrong woman to judge how children should be brought up. You may be a believer in strict discipline—of the children-should-be-seen-

and-not-heard school. You may be one of those many grand-parents who think that their daughters are incompetent women who do everything wrong.

I trust you realize that if the parents of your grand-child are not on the side of the child, that child will not find happiness now or later on in life. But, on the other hand, lavish gifts of radio sets and bicycles don't insure happiness for a child, just as Cadillacs and Rolls Royces never in-creased the true inner happiness of an adult by one iota. When things come too easily, they are not appreciated. That's why a good psychotherapist will refuse to take a patient without fees, knowing that the patient will value at nothing what he gets for nothing.

My youngster is just crazy about jazz. He is the leader of a band that practices in our house. My husband and I are at a point when we can stand it no longer. We are simply going out of our minds with the constant racket of his prac-ticing all day on a saxophone, and the band practicing three times a week. How does one solve a problem like this?

The boy says he has no other place to meet and prac-tice. If it were my house, I'd get rid of the racket by hiring some small room outside, and I'd gladly pay the rent.

But there's always the question of money. Can you afford to pay for a practice room?

I personally sympathize with you—for I abhor some of the noise that's called music. My school has its own jazz band, but luckily, the band practices in a room that is a good distance from my sitting room.

But to make the jazz band taboo would be a crime

against the boy, and would lead to a tenseness in the home that would be unbearable. You can't ban jazz or rock and roll or any other kind of modern expression just because it isn't to your taste.

I can see no other solution but the hired hall. But if you can't possibly afford the expense, I can only suggest ear plugs and resignation. In the home of a professional piano teacher, the family simply has to bear the din.

When there is a conversation in our home my daughter gets attention by shouting. My husband is constantly in a stew about this. He just shouts her down. We tell her it is bad manners, unattractive, etc., but it all falls on deaf ears. Have you any solution?

Yes, one that I have often used in my school. *"Mary, you aren't talking loudly enough. Go on, raise your voice."* It usually works.

The repressive way is just futile and a waste of time. It looks to me as if your daughter feels inferior, a nobody in the family. Her shouting may mean: *"Look, folks, you can't neglect me; I'll damn well make you hear."* And it might well be a perpetual protest against suppression by you.

But why worry about what, after all, is a minor affair. Do you worry about your daughter's indoctrination at school or in church? Do you ever sit down calmly and ask yourself: *Why is my kid rebellious and unhappy?*

Go deep, folks, go deep and stop worrying about things that are only outer symptoms of inner conflicts. Try to get down to brass tacks, to depths of life, and beyond the silly conventional things that are ephemeral and unimportant.

That poor kid of yours has some grievance, some protest, some misery that she is hiding from you.

Shouting can be a disguise; the timid man when attacked may shout to hide his terror. We cannot cure anything by attacking the symptoms. You, her parents, should try to make your home a happy place for your child.

My son of five is very much involved with a serial TV program at 6 P.M. every day. The TV set is in the living room. His father comes home every day around six, dog-tired and yearning for quiet and relaxation. My husband is very much annoyed by the cops-and-robbers program. How does one reconcile these conflicting interests?

Not knowing the geography of the house, I cannot know if the TV set could be placed in another room, say in the kitchen or in a bedroom. Unfortunately, Daddy's irritation will convey itself to the boy, and the lad might possibly equate TV pleasure with parental annoyance.

Thousands of homes have similar problems. My own TV set is in our living room. I have often to watch a program that others want to see but I don't. But then again, I can move into another room. The curse of every family is the TV program; for the most part, the adults want to see a good play while the juniors want pop music or a serial.

In a free family, there is a give and take. Junior likes Batman on the TV; Senior wants drama or football. What to do? My wife and I are in that same position with our daughter. We solve it by give and take. We say, "At seven, you can have your jazz musicians; at eight, I'm going to see a play by Shaw."

To answer the question directly: there are but two ways as far as I can see; either move the set to another room, or tell Junior he can't have the TV on every night. Moving the set is the better way because denying him his beloved program can mean to Junior *"They don't love me."* That estimate can lead to far worse things than Dad's annoyance with a stupid superman film.

My daughter is always borrowing my clothes. She has an adequate wardrobe of her own, but she always seems to want my things. Sometimes when she knows something is new or expensive, she just borrows it without asking for permission. Should I punish her?

No, definitely no. Your daughter may have such a high opinion of you that she identifies herself with you to the extent of even wanting to wear your clothes. Or she may have a strong fixation on her father, and feel—not think— *"I want to take mother's place in his affections."*

True, the girl is indulging in license. She is taking things without permission that do not belong to her. But you must query *why* she is acting in this way. Really, Mother, why *doesn't* your girl ask your permission?

To me, it looks as if your relationship isn't one of love. The mere fact that you talk of punishment indicates this. It could be that the girl is subconsciously thinking: *"If I can't get Mother's love, I'll get her hate. A good way to get some reaction from Mommy is to wear her clothes."*

Our clothes are, as it were, parts of our personality, but so are our children. An incident like this, or even several such episodes, would not make a balanced mother go off the deep end. The more one values clothes, the less one is a balanced adult. The conventional Englishman with his striped trousers and his absurd bowler hat values his appearance so much because he hasn't enough inside himself to value. To overvalue clothes suggests a lack of interest in more important things in life.

Punishment and raging won't help a whit; on the contrary, such measures will afford the girl proof that she is not loved enough. But it is not difficult to effectively treat a situation, without hate or punishment, if the relationship between mother and daughter is a natural one. When Bobby borrows one of my wrenches and does not return it, I don't scruple to forcibly tell him that I want the wrench back; but my telling has no hate, nor anger, nor morality in it. Next day, Bobby may tell me off for coming late to a lesson. He often does. And that same feeling can be the rule in a family when the gulf between parent and child is not an unbridgeable one, when no fear has been instilled into the young.

Make your home a happy place for your child, and you'll be surprised how quickly so many problems will disappear.

SELF-REGULATION

You have so often in your book, SUMMERHILL, mentioned self-regulation. What exactly does self-regulation mean?

Self-regulation depends so much on the mother's own psychology, on her philosophy, on her values. No child can be self-regulated when a mother is more interested in things than in her child. Self-regulation is foreign to the sort of

mother who flies into a temper if some silly vase is broken,
or one who wants to impress her neighbors by having a
nice, well-behaved boy or girl. No mother with a complex
about sex and excrement can have a self-regulated child.
The term postulates a balanced woman, a relaxed woman.

I seem to be painting a picture of an ideal mother who
never was on land or sea. Yet what I am trying to say is that
a child cannot be more self-regulated than his mother is.
Every mother must regulate herself first before she can rear
a self-regulated child. She must drop all conventional ideas
about cleanliness, untidiness, noise, swearing, sex play, destruction of toys, etc. Many toys should be destroyed consciously by a healthy child. No moralist, no follower of
religious rites, no disciplinarian can have a self-regulated
child. *Self-regulation means behavior that springs from the
self—not from outside compulsion.* The molded child has no
self; he is only a replica of his parents.

To permit self-regulation, one does not need to be educated nor cultured. I think of Mary, a plain woman in a
Scottish fishing village. Mary had wonderful placidity; she
never fussed, never stormed; she was instinctively on the
side of her boys and girls; they knew that she approved of
them whatever they did. Mary as a mother was a comfy
warm hen with her chicks around her; she had a natural gift
of giving out love without making it possessive love. Here
was a simple soul who never heard of psychology or self-
regulation, yet who fully practiced self-regulation. She followed her emotions in dealing with the family, and did not
act according to any set rules of child rearing. Mind you,
she enjoyed better conditions than a mother living in a
Philadelphia flat. Her children were out of doors much of
the time. Indoors, there were no expensive gadgets to pro-

tect from infant hands, no radios, no TV sets, no electric irons. The family had no costly clothes to keep free from dirt. There was a simple give and take, and an absence of parental bossiness. The children grew like weeds, free from excessive cultivation, and nurtured in love. Mary knew what to expect from a child, much as she knew what to expect from a calf. She didn't expect a cucumber to sprout beautiful flowers, nor did she expect her three-year-old to be clean and considerate. What was tolerated in a five-year-old was not tolerated in a 10-year-old. Mary loved her children but she also loved herself—respected herself, and would never permit any of her brood to exploit her kindliness. She called a spade a spade. The kids knew she was on the level; they knew she couldn't be pushed all over the lot, but over all, they knew that here was a mother who never exploited them, who loved them, and never pushed them to fulfill impossible goals. Here was true self-regulation—a home without pressure.

"All very well," says the American city mother, "but I don't live in the country."

I suppose that the question hinges on how much you really love your child. Your two-year-old will behave badly if he feels he is in a strained environment, that you're always saying "No, don't!" He will sense that life for him is one long training period.

You should never try to make your child clean in a sanitary sense, shoving him on the pot to train him. If the pot is there, he will, in good time, come to use it himself. If he dislikes some particular food, you must on no account force him to eat it, or even persuade him to eat it. If and when he touches his genitals, you should smile approval.

What about his tantrums? His hitting his little sister?

His smashing things? It is useless to try to reason with a child of two, for he cannot grasp cause and effect. It is hopeless to say when he pulls the cat's tail: "How would you like it if I pulled your nose?" There are times when you have to say no, times when you have to take the child away from a smaller weeping sister whom he has wantonly slugged, times when you must say "Leave that alone." The placid mother will *know* what to do and what to say. But the mother whose voice and whose hand scare her child will only create an increase of naughtiness.

Self-regulation is intangible; no one can teach it. There are so few children who have been reared in self-regulation from infancy on. I see in them less aggression, more tolerance, looser bodies, freer spirits. They are not likely to submit to conditioning by anti-life moralists.

But self-regulation does not mean that a child should not be protected. When a mother writes to ask me if it would be against self-regulation if she puts up a fireguard, I sigh.

One of the most harrassed mothers is she who is raising a four-year-old and lives on a busy thoroughfare. Often, she has to forget all about self-regulation and grab in fear at her wandering child. Cars, bicycles, inflammable goods, ditches—these all make self-regulation far from easy for many an anxious mother. But, if mother is only anxious about her child's safety and doesn't interfere with him in other ways, there is much hope for the child.

Lots of people are mouthing the words you wrote about Summerhill but do not appear to me to do anything about it. They seem to have got Summerhill in their heads but not

in their guts. I know parents who quote the book with
enthusiasm and then curb the freedom of their children.
Any comment?

Yes, it is quite true that some parents appreciate the
idea of freedom intellectually, but not emotionally. They
are the ones who say: *Freedom is fine, but . . . !* Often the
but means: *How will free children fit into an unfree society?*
Often the but means: *Will my daughter seek free love?*
When the but doesn't connote fear, it indicates puritanism.

I recall Wilhelm Stekel's story of his analysis of a boy of
17, the son of a psychiatrist. The boy felt a great guilt because he had had sexual intercourse with his sister. At the
end of the analysis, the father consulted Stekel in the boy's
presence. "Well Doctor, what was wrong with the lad?"

Stekel answered that he could never betray a patient's
confidence, not even to a father.

The boy said: "I'd like father to know," so Stekel told
all.

The father laughed. "Of course I understand—the old
incest complex."

Next day, when the boy came to Stekel, his face was
black and blue. His psychiatrist father had taken him home
and given him a very cruel beating.

Later on, the father himself came to Stekel for analysis.
Stekel discovered that the father was really in love with his
own daughter, and had been actuated by jealousy when he
had beaten his son.

Here is a good example of one accepting a situation
intellectually but rejecting it emotionally. After hearing
that story about 45 years ago, I have been chary of telling a
parent any secrets unearthed by talking to a boy or girl.

As for those who mouth words about freedom, Reich called them the truth peddlers. I know them. They are not insincere; they are usually young idealists who seize on part of a message, and adapt that portion in line with their own complexes. Question: Don't we all do just that?

The applicant for a job at my school whom I will not employ is the man who comes raving to me about Summerhill. *"All my life I have been seeking this paradise."* Invariably, such a man or woman is not a successful teacher. For Summerhill is not an ideal place, and in two weeks the dream is shattered. I steer clear of starry-eyed teachers.

In the end, a man must be judged by his actions. It is futile to go around talking glibly about freedom for children if one does nothing about it. I feel that Krishnamurti should have spent his life with children instead of going around the world lecturing to middle-class women, some of whom I fear used his message to bolster up their useless existence. Beware of preachers whether they be Billy Grahams or political agitators. I comfort my conscience when I go lecturing by knowing that I lecture on what I have done, and not on what I am doing. One should expect a writer and a preacher to practice what he preaches. Bishops who bless battleships, please note.

The only gospel a man should preach is one that is his own, although it is hard to know how much one has taken from others. Like me with my getting self-government from Homer Lane and self-regulation from Reich.

No man is an island. But I am glad that Orson Bean does not call his school on 15th Street, New York, a Summerhill school. He will go his own way.

Anti-Life Attitudes

MANNERS

How can children learn manners if they are not told how to behave at table, or how to act when meeting people? I agree that manners are not natural. Therefore, should they not be taught?

The question is really: *Should we teach our children etiquette?*

I recall the first time I encoutered a finger-bowl at a posh dinner party. One man drank from his; I was wary enough to watch what others did.

It is good to know which table tools to use; but of course, etiquette differs in each country. In Britain, no gentleman will drink if he has any food in his mouth; but on the Continent, this social rule does not obtain. I once committed a gaffe by seating myself on the sofa in a German house; later, I was told that in a German home the sofa was always reserved for important guests.

Doffing my hat to a woman is a gesture which covers up the fact that in our patriarchal civilization a woman is held to be inferior. Our special manners toward women show a compensation for that belief.

Yes, it is best to know your etiquette in our conventional world. But manners are a different story. Good manners mean thinking of others. Manners cannot be taught. In my school, we do not teach etiquette; if a child licks his plate, no one cares—indeed, no one notices. We never groom a child to say *Thank You* or *Good Morning*. But when a boy mocked a new lad who was lame, the other children called a special meeting and the offender was told by the community, and in no uncertain terms, that the school did not relish bad manners.

A free child develops natural manners; as he grows older, he is wise enough to pick up the surface politeness that had best be termed *etiquette*.

If a child is not polite in the ordinary sense, he will undoubtedly offend certain people. Won't their rejection of him or displeasure prove damaging to the child?

What is politeness? It is thinking of others and their feelings. Young children are primarily interested in themselves; the adult egoist is the man who has never grown up.

A disciplined child is polite to adults if he is afraid of them; a free child acquires a natural politeness without sacrificing his sincerity. If a child is always discourteous it is because he has been reared wrongly, has developed resentment against grown-ups. Think of the bad effect on a child who is told *"Kiss Grandmother";* or of the resentment the child feels when he is told *"Child, thank Aunt Mary for her nice present."*

Wise parents and teachers never ask for politeness. Discourtesy is bred by demanding parents. Mrs. Smith says, "I'd hate Mrs. Green next door to think that my kids haven't been properly brought up." Mrs. Smith seeks to conciliate the neighbors at her child's expense.

I think the word *gratitude* should be erased from the dictionary. People who demand gratitude are foolish. My good friend, Henry Miller, wrote me saying that he was making a lot of money from the publication of *The Tropic of Cancer.* "I think that Summerhill should have some," he said, and he sent me $1,000. But my feelings towards Henry are not feelings of gratitude; they are feelings of warmth for a very dear, dear man. I have no idea what sort of feelings I should have if an unknown John Smith sent me a million bucks. I am sure the word *gratitude* would not cover such feelings.

My dear parent, leave your children to find their own measure of politeness. Give them love, and they will automatically be polite. But if you nag your children with rules of behavior, you may well be laying the groundwork within them for inconsideration to others.

My boy has never been taught manners. He says *Thank You* and *Please* of his own accord. He is considerate of other people. But for some reason he tends to grab food with his fingers. My wife and I have sat by complacently hoping that he will outgrow this, but he continues in his miserable ways. Frankly, it has become a matter of disgust to us; and besides, we wonder if he won't become permanently habituated in this respect, to his own and our embarrassment in later years. What do you think?

Is he 5 or 10 or 15? Of course, he will grow out of it in time. When he takes his first love home to lunch, he won't grab the food with his fingers.

I would do nothing about the habit so long as he was touching what he himself was to eat. I should certainly protest if he shoved his finger into the apple pie that was my portion of the meal.

He may have a complex about conventionality. Our eating habits are stylized. Why should we not eat peas with a knife, or pour our tea into the saucer to cool it? Why cannot we take up cheese with our fingers instead of putting it on a biscuit with a knife? We eat apples and pears by hand, so why not sausages or pork pies? I think the boy has got something there. Mind, I am not excluding the idea that his unconscious motive may be just to annoy the old folks.

You say in your letter that you and your wife believe in the principle of not imposing any kind of learning or strictures on the boy. But since when has this been so? Were you character formers before you heard of Summerhill? Did you, in fact, dominate the boy when he was very young. Did you, some years later, say to the boy: *"You are free to do what you like?"* If so, he is doing it. If it were my problem, I'd say nothing.

I am reminded of a wonderful display of good manners I once witnessed. The village minister invited a workman to lunch. The dish was mince. The workman at once began to shovel it in with his knife. The minister took up his knife and wielded it with gusto. Of course, I followed suit.

DUTY AND RESPONSIBILITY

Why should a child do only what he likes to do? How can he face life which demands a thousand unpleasant duties?

Childhood is not adulthood; childhood is playhood and no child ever gets enough play. When a child has played enough he will start to work and face difficulties, and do a good job even when it involves a lot of unpleasant work.

Most men hate their work. I have often asked folks: "If you won a fortune, would you keep your job?" Artists, doctors, some schoolmasters, musicians, farmers, and other creative people say yes. Many others say they would give up their work—mostly laborers, shop assistants, clerks, truck drivers, and factory workers who stand by an assembly line and have no feeling about the completed product. For most jobs are of no real interest; the young, especially, dislike them.

Children reared in freedom can tackle unpleasant duties—but such children never make an obsession of the work. What I mean is that the free child doesn't get overly involved in anger and hate against those who demand these duties. If a young man or young woman experiences inner freedom, tasks are not overly resented.

Last week my son, Tommy, got on his motorcycle, raced through the town and collided with a parked automobile, causing damage estimated at $150. We just don't have the income that can afford to pay for this kind of unforeseen expense. But, of course, we have to foot this particular bill. What should be done? Should we take the money week-by-week out of Tommy's allowance? Should we insist on his selling his motorcycle to raise money to pay for the damage? Or what?

If you make Tommy sell his motorbike to pay for the damage, he will resent it strongly and take it as a proof of your lack of love for him. But I don't see why he should not help to pay the damages out of his allowances. After all, he has to face reality, and he has got to learn that his own carelessness cannot be paid for by his parents.

But I don't know his age, or what sort of boy he is. If 12 or so, he might look upon paying up as a punishment· and resent it; but if he is 17, he should be able to see the rationale of his sharing the cost.

I was widowed when my son was 6. I am compelled to work for a living and the going has been rough. My boy is now 16, in high school, and doing well. There is not the slightest prospect of my supporting him through college. I'd like him to stop school now and get a job to help support his two younger sisters. Have I the right to insist that he become the man of the family at his age?

I don't know what prospects the boy has if he stays on at school, but I just feel that it would be wrong to make him the man in the house at his age. I guess that any job he got at this stage wouldn't be a very good one.

I·think you should struggle on for a year or two and give the lad a chance to decide for himself what he wants to do in life. If you forced the boy to leave school and he resented having to go out to work, the family atmosphere wouldn't be a very happy one, would it?

No, let *him* decide, I say.

My wife is a slave to our children—she picks up their clothes after them, irons for them, and does all their household chores. I keep telling her that she is making irresponsible brats out of them, but she says a little kindness and attention never spoiled a child. Who is right?

The way it sounds to me your wife is right.

Since childhood is playhood, the child's right is to play and play. You should expect that. Your timetable for your children is not natural. In Summerhill, we do not ask children to do chores. The older ones do a few tasks because they want their rooms to look nice. Younger children simply do not care. But if left alone, these same children may well be concerned *when they grow older* about how their premises look.

Of course, the situation in a home is different. I sympathize with the mother whose adolescent children leave her to wash up the dishes and sweep the floors. With adolescents, she certainly has the right to say that they must take their part in the work, but with smaller children, no. Part of the trouble arises from the different standards of young and old. An untidy room does not mean a thing to most children; and I go so far as to say that trim spic-and-span quarters do not count too much with many men. If children wash up voluntarily—fine; but continual nagging of a young child means a lack of paternal love.

Generally speaking, a child up to seven will tidy up and do work; but in two years, he will shun all housework. I have often seen adolescent girls grumble at being asked to do chores; but when mother went off for a week's vacation, they kept the house as neat as a pin.

I suspect that every child unconsciously feels that the job of the grown-ups is to do things for him. They grow out of this stage in time—if not badgered. With teenagers, I counsel forbearance. The prudent parent will not make excessive demands—excessive from a psychological viewpoint.

And, oh, husband, do you do your share of those chores? You should, you know.

My son, 15, avoids all chores. He always has an objection when he is asked to mow the lawn or to deliver a package, or to do anything else we request. He feels we are infringing on his rights. We can't afford a gardener, nor a messenger service nor any other extra expenditures. My wife and I feel that a boy of his age should have a sense of responsibility, that we have the right to call on him for certain things that are within his power. Yet we hesitate to apply pressure. For one thing, he is our only child and we fear to alienate him. But on the other hand, we have grave bouts with our consciences and fear that we are coddling him by not insisting that he help out in home affairs.

Oh, the thousands of parents who have the same problem! Jenny won't help wash up when she is home for holidays; Peter loafs around and won't even fill the coal scuttle. In most families the situation is the same. The young hate chores, and have not attained the sense of duty that makes adults do unwelcome tasks. To me this means that infancy lasts much longer than most people think it does.

An analogous problem is that of adolescents lying about in bed late in the morning. We may bawl them out, but we should at the same time try to see their point of view. Perhaps adolescents live more in fantasy than we imagine. Real life means dull chores at home, and the young are not ready to face the realities of life. The 15-year-old girl who sleeps late may be wanting to avoid what for her would be unpleasant household duties. True, most adolescents are dragooned into doing the dull tasks, either by lectures or by fear of punishment; but the moment the outer compulsion is absent, the true ungrownupness of childhood shows itself and the adolescent is back to babyhood and irresponsibility again. Cats and dogs have no chores to do. Perhaps the adolescent who avoids responsibility feels in some way that his parents have kept him as a pet.

The unspoken thought is: *My dad and mom are there, and it is their job to run the house.* Yes, it is indeed a tough problem, for as you rightly surmise, bossing the child can lead to alienation. In a family that had real freedom in it, no such result would follow. My wife says to our daughter: "Come on. Your turn to wash up," without in any way risking defiance. Only in an authoritarian family will alienation ensue.

Forced labor is always wrong. If a boss has to keep on telling an employee what to do and how to do it, he would do best to fire him. Good work comes only when the worker is willing. The compulsion should come from the job, not from the boss or the parent. The only honor worth having is the personal satisfaction of having done a job well and sincerely.

One interesting feature in most families is that if the parents are away on vacation, the adolescents will cook and wash up and sweep the floors. For the moment, necessity has made the children adult. But the moment the old folks return, the antagonism to chores comes into play.

A wise society would not ask anyone under 20 to do a stroke of work, for infancy lasts far into the teens. Childhood is playhood—we should face that fact. So, worried parents, sigh and reach for the dishcloth, and remember that your child's standards are different from yours. To many an adolescent, an untidy room means nothing—he simply doesn't see it.

Parents, however, must refrain from exploiting children . . . . *"Fetch the hammer, Billy."* Fine if Billy is helping you mend a table, but not so fine if Billy is making a boat or reading a book.

RESPECT

How should a child be taught respect for his parents?

What on earth does the word *respect* mean? I think the main ingredient of that word is fear, as in the case of children who respect their stern teachers. My dictionary calls respect *esteem for merit, honor, to esteem highly*. Okay, if your children do not think that you are meritorious or honorable or worthy of esteem, what can you do about it? *Force* them to think you're great?

My pupils do not respect me. I never demand respect. Today, a girl of ten called me a silly fool. So what? That was her opinion this morning and she's entitled to it. Nor did her statement mean she didn't love me.

There is something undeveloped about parents who demand respect. Obviously, they have failed to inspire love in their children, and so they demand an inferior substitute. Parents who are really fair and square with their children do not require respect.

How can a child respect a nagging mother or a roaring father? How can a child respect parents whom he hears lying? How can a child respect a mother who dares not stand up to a bullying husband?

I respect Bertrand Russell because of his philosophy, his humanitarianism, but that respect has no fear or envy in it. If you want to be respected by your child, act in such a manner that the respect comes naturally—which means deservedly—and not because your child fears reprisal.

My youngster, Donald, pays scant respect to his grandparents. My husband and I never demanded respect. What we want is love, and we think we're getting it from Donald. But I am utterly abashed by the indifference which Donald shows his grandparents, both my parents and my husband's parents. They are scandalized by his disinterest and lack of courtesy. Is there anything I can say to the boy?

I sympathize with you, with the grandparents, and with Donald. Grandparents are usually of two sorts: some spoil the child, alleging that the parents have no idea how to rear their own children; the other sort sees youth as a menace to all they believe in. They abhor the horrid, long-haired, slang-speaking gadabouts who have no interest other than pop music and parties.

It looks, in this case, as if the oldsters belong to the second sort. Donald probably resents their interference and their moralizing. There is a great gulf between a boy of 10 and a grandparent of 70. The old and the young just don't talk the same language, nor have they the same interests. Most grandparents are anchored to a bygone era. Styles and ways to which they are not accustomed may appear dissolute.

When my parents were alive, I wrote home regularly and my letters were "weather" ones—I would write and say, "The sun has been out all day. How's the weather back home?" I had to think up what might interest them.

If Donald does not like his grannies, I don't see what can be done about it. Talking to him would be wasting one's breath. Young children have a natural honesty. If Donald knew that his grandparents would leave him a million dollars if he approved of them, he could not change his attitude.

All I can suggest is that Donald be kept as far away from his grandparents as possible.

When my child is frustrated, he gets angry. He even becomes abusive and says: "You mean thing, you witch." Shall I permit him to live out his anger, or should he be restrained from abusing me? The fact is I feel very hurt when I hear him characterize me in this way.

To restrain him will do no good; it will simple mean that his hate turns inside and festers.

A better way would be for you to join in the fun and call him all the names you can think of—but not in anger, of course. There's one good side to this picture—the boy isn't afraid to call you names. Good!

You feel hurt because you feel guilty . . . *"Had I shown him more love, he wouldn't react with hate like he does."* A child should respect his parents. Dear me!

My advice to you is to learn to laugh along with your boy. Humor and hate do not go together. The lad may be abnormally honest, for there must be a few million children who would sometimes like to call their mother something that rhymes with *witch* but don't dare to. His hate, ventilated, will expend itself; but if he is spanked, lectured, or restrained, that hate may remain there for a very long time.

CONVENTIONALISM

My niece, Mary Lou, wants to become a dancer. Her parents are appalled. They equate such a profession with waywardness. What can I say to them to convince them that my niece is seeking a worthwhile career?

Poor Mary Lou! Her parents apparently still live in the Victorian era. I am afraid that nothing you can say to them will help Mary Lou. They may turn a born Pavlova into an office secretary, and frustrate her for life. They sound just bone selfish.

Their fear of waywardness suggests that to them sex is evil and wrong, for the word *waywardness* signifies looseness in morals. I don't know what to say about dead parents like them.

When We Dead Awaken says the play title. Dead folks never awaken.

I'm afraid little Mary Lou, like thousands of her sisters, is to be sacrificed to a puritanism that is long out-of-date.

DISHONESTY

Am I justified in sometimes lying to my daughter?

I can imagine an occasion on which you would have to lie to her. Suppose she is seriously ill in the hospital after an automobile accident in which her father was killed. She asks how her daddy is; you say he is fine. What else *can* you say?

We all tell white lies. Miss Brown sings and I think her voice is dreadful; but I smile and thank her. White lies are nearly always told to prevent someone's being hurt. A husband is asked by his wife how he likes her new hat which she bought at a sale. It is hideous. But paid for and nonreturnable. What *should* he say, if he isn't a cad.

I think we should abolish references. No employer likes to mar a man's future by giving him a bad reference, and that is why when I advertise for a teacher I usually say: "No references."

I once had a teacher I wanted to get rid of, but moral cowardice kept me from telling him to go. At last, he applied for another job and asked me for a reference. I gave him a glowing one. He was so pleased with my appreciation that he cancelled his application and stayed on with me.

I like the story of the man who sought a job as janitor. His previous employer wrote that he was generally honest. The personnel manager wondered what the adverb meant; he phoned the ex-employer and asked him to explain the phrase, "generally honest."

"I used the word *generally* in its proper context as meaning not particularly," came the answer.

If you say to your child: "Answer the phone, dear, and if it's Mrs. Jones, say I'm not in," you are not doing as much damage as you do when your child knows you are living a lie, pretending that all is well in your marriage when you and your husband are hating each other. I have often said it is better to divorce than to live a lie. More than once I have seen children grow happier after the divorce, for they were no longer living in a dishonest, lying atmosphere.

I know that many parents seek to be models to their children. Many a parent is chagrined when his child discovers something about his past——that Daddy at school was cordially despised when he was a kid, that Mother was always near the bottom of her class. I have known many mothers who wouldn't tell their family their age, fathers who would never tell their wives what their income was. Possibly most parental lies are defensive lies, lies to preserve the image of the perfect father, the perfect mother. That is so wrong. Your child should be aware of your virtues and your weaknesses. That is healthier by far. Your child should like you for what you are—he should not like someone who doesn't exist. Every small boy thinks that his father could hold off six men: it takes a brave father to candidly admit he couldn't fight anyone.

One of the worst lies is the statement: "Now when I was a boy I didn't steal." Any child who hears this rot will intuitively know that his father must have been cowed as a youngster or that his father has a convenient forgettery.

Most parental lies spring from the nonsensical notion that a parent must never confess to being human. How many fathers could give an honest answer to a child if he were asked if he ever masturbated? How many mothers will confess to having had a sex life before marriage? And the modern child will sometimes ask such embarrassing questions.

Yes, it is in the sex sphere that so many parents lie. Where do babies come from? How are babies made? Easy questions, really, to answer if the parent is honest. I think almost all parental lies are unnecessary, and that almost all such lies boomerang. Lies do subtle, and not so subtle, damage to both the parent and the child.

DISCRIMINATION

I live in the deep South in a small town outside of Atlanta. I commute to work and have a good job. My wife and I are both college educated, yet our children, Nancy 11 and Bob 13, have a strong feeling of inferiority because they are Negro. Everyone in the neighborhood, whether openly or not, believes we are inferior and treats us as inferior, but I have always felt that neither my wife nor I have permitted this atmosphere to penetrate the home. Here we are with two wonderful children, each of whom thinks he is somewhat cursed because he has been born with a black skin.

This is not a question—just a sad statement. I have never been in the deep South, but what I have read about it sickens me. I don't know if the two children go to a mixed or a segregated school, don't know if they play with white children. It seems that white children are indoctrinated with hate from their cradle days, for children have little or no natural feeling about color.

In Summerhill, no child seems to notice if another is black or white. In a lecture tour of South Africa in 1936, I, of course, saw the hateful attitude of white to black, and I was told that the Calvinist Church there accepted the situation on the ground that the Bible consigns the black man to be a hewer of wood and a drawer of water. What rot!

It would take too long to go into the deep reasons behind the color complex, but roughly I think the Negroes stand symbolically for all that the white man hates in himself. They are black—impure; white is purity. In food, too, there is a call for white rice and white bread, as if by denaturing the fine natural product, the food were being purified. A poultry farmer in New Jersey once told me that he had to stock Leghorns only because few New Yorkers would buy a brown egg that came from a Rhode Island Red.

At bottom, of course, all haters seek a whipping boy; Hitler, the Jews; Americans, the Communists. In Britain, too, after the influx of so many West Indians, we now have a color complex.

How can Negro children escape this mass hate and intolerance? It is an appalling situation. These two young children will have to face it. I hope they have the integrity and courage to see through the inhumanity of their white neighbors. I am sure that these white neighbors go to church and call themselves Christians.

I wish I could give you some practical advice. I cannot. Any more than I could give advice to an anti-Communist living in East Berlin. There is seldom any way out of a mass trap—only personal integrity and bravery.

My girl is 15, and attends a high school here in our small Midwestern town. Last week she came home in tears. She had been blackballed by the sorority she had set her heart on because she was Jewish. There was little that I could say to bolster her injured feelings. Somehow, it comes through to her that where there's smoke, there's fire. She has the notion that there must be something wrong with Jews or else they wouldn't be considered in such a dismal light by so many people. I am afraid of the psychological effect. What can I do to bolster her sense of self-worth? What can I do to prove to her that the attitudes to which she has been subjected are pernicious?

This beastly business of anti-Semitism again. So many Jewish children suffer in school and society. I have had a girl pupil of 14 scream: "I'd give anything not to be a Jewess." It is not only in America that the hateful abomination flourishes. We have it in Britain where some tennis and golf clubs blackball Jews. Why, we have it in some Jews; I have known more than one Hebrew who was anti-Semitic.

The home should be able to do something about such

a matter. If it is a home with love in it, you should talk freely about the whole situation, helping your daughter to realize that the better-than-thou sorority has no significance in her life, that her school sisters are narrow little people with warped souls. You should bring everything to the surface, and give the girl a wide view of life, life that has nothing to do with creed or class or race.

Many people in minority groups feel inferior: blacks in Rhodesia, Jews in Germany, Puerto Ricans in New York. When he treks south to live and work, no Scot thinks he is inferior to an Englishman. The Scots have a pride of race; the best Jews have a similar pride. That lass should be encouraged to believe, not that she is one of the Chosen People, but that she is one of a race that has enriched the world with a Freud, an Einstein, a Jonas Salk, with great sculptors and great painters. The girl should learn that anyone who is anti-Semitic is a poor, undeveloped, frustrated person who cannot love, and who can only hate. She should feel superior to the stupid girls who scorn her. I hope she will soon come to see how valueless and bitchy they are.

We are all passive about the world's evils. We know that children in Vietnam are being roasted alive by flame-throwers and napalm bombs; we know that blacks are beaten up in American and South African jails. We shut our eyes to the massive cruelty in the world, and we only show our indignation and wrath when the papers publish a story of a dog's being beaten or starved. One black sheep challenging the whole flock emits but a feeble baa-baa. The ultimate remedy for a sick world are many challengers of power, many challengers of hate, and many challengers of out-of-date morals.

School

What can I do about the American education system? My daughter is 14 and she hates her school. She says that originality is frowned on, that the teaching is dull, that some of her teachers are sarcastic. What can I do to save her from being pressurized into a conforming woman who pursues status and big cars and expensive houses and a dead psychology?

Madam, I wish I knew what you could do. If you can afford it, you can send your daughter to a private school, more along the lines you believe in. If you cannot afford a private school, your poor daughter is in the soup. Only an enlightened and happy home can counteract the baleful indoctrination and deadness of the usual school. The saddest letters I write are in reply to boys and girls who write telling me how they hate their schools. I answer saying that, however much they hate the lessons and the way they are presented, the damn system is there, and the only thing to do is to grit your teeth and accept it and get through it as quickly as possible.

The children who write me are challenging children, but the vast majority of children never challenge; they accept the indoctrination. The acceptance makes it easier for them later to adapt themselves to our materialistic society. And so the worship of the almighty dollar goes on from one generation to another. Alas! Character-molded parents haven't the guts nor the inclination to protest against a stultifying school system.

Cold comfort for you, madam, and for your daughter.

Nor will it be any comfort for you to know that there are thousands of parents who have your problem. We have the same problem in Britain; only so far, we haven't arrived at the fatuous American system of giving tests to every prospective condidate for a job—tests that apparently strip a man or woman naked. An American spokesman for this sort of thing said on our TV the other night that they even investigate a man's wife, for it is felt that if she is a nag or a neurotic, the man won't be able to concentrate on his work.

It is at least satisfying to know that many parents and many children in America are rejecting the rat race. They are beginning to evaluate the mad system of forced study and competitive examinations for what they are. Call it what you will, but don't call it education!

My girl is now seven. She has been in school for one year. She hates it. She says her teachers are mean to her. I have spoken to her teacher, and my impression is that she is no shining light in the firmament of education.

But the law here in Massachusetts insists that my child go to school; and the local authorities say that my child must go to the particular school she now attends; and the principal of the school says that it would disrupt the whole curriculum if he transferred my little girl to another class, since that would open the door for every other child in that school to ask to be transferred to another class.

So my little girl is stuck in her hated classroom. I write to plead with you for some words of advice. What can I do or say to the child to make her lot easier? I fear, among other things, that she may develop a lifelong hatred against learning or school work.

Oh, these schools! I cannot count the number of letters I have had from school kids in America saying that they hate their schools.

This poor child is the victim of organization—organization that puts the individual child into a category so as to make the life of the teacher as easy as possible. It is simply scandalous that any child of any age should say: "I hate my school."

I fear mass production has come to stay, both in commerce and in education. Stamp all children in the same die; educate them so that they will never challenge anything. Let the little blighters suffer in the process; they don't matter. All that matters is the compulsive system, the molding of character so that all will think the same way, dress the same way, and speak the same way. Uniformity first! And thousands of poor, helpless children cry and are wretched in their factory schools.

Always the same story. . . . "I hate my school. My teachers make every lesson dull. They don't accept answers that aren't in the book. They insist on lots of silly rules, like not speaking in the corridors when we change rooms."

To persecute children in this way is appalling. Young lives crushed by undeveloped, pip-squeak authorities! A natural love of learning warped by dull teaching! It makes one cry. I fear that the majority of teachers hate their work, hate their children, hate themselves.

Such egocentrism! The math teacher thinks that math is the center of all life—for him nothing else counts. The geography teacher believes that knowing the capital of Madagascar is more important than playing baseball.

You, poor woman, are up against the system that not only tolerates narrow-minded teachers but apparently selects them. Education is bunk, until we fill our schools with men and women who love and understand children.

Bernard Shaw once said: "He who can, does: he who cannot, teaches."

How many teachers are doers? How many teachers of English ever write a good book? How many art teachers produce a picture good enough to be exhibited? I believe that many of my old pupils do not want to become teachers because they are too well balanced, too alive to enter a system where they would be expected to become stuffed shirts demanding obedience and deference.

But what can you, as a mother, do? The only thing you can do is to try to counteract the stupid system by giving your child freedom at home.

My two children, a girl of 9 and a boy of 10, just hate public school. I can't afford to send them to a private school, and the law does not permit me to withdraw them from school. What can I say when I too believe that their school is unprogressive, and to a large extent, ineffective. Suppose I agree that their teacher is a dunce, will it do any good if I tell them this? Or will it make them unhappy?

They seem to be unhappy enough already; your telling them the teacher is a dunce won't make any difference. This question bothers me, for it is one I get in scores of letters from the U.S.A.; the question bothers me because I cannot think of a solution.

The Establishment, the compact majority, believe in the system; the Establishment has the power to enforce it. The deadness and boredom of certain school subjects conveys itself to the teachers; and so, schools are filled with narrow, self-important men and women whose horizon is bounded by the blackboard and the textbook. If you want to realize how dead most teachers are, read any educational journal.

Reforms usually come about three generations after they are first proposed. One day, there will be sane laws about homosexuality, abortion, legal punishment—and education. Today, the minority just has to sigh and bear all the idiocies we call schooling. The awful tragedy is that the mass of children accept the insane standards of the schools, but at the terrible price of losing their inner freedom. Our schools produce a race of dead souls who are at the mercy of the politicians, the war-makers, and the profit-seekers.

You, poor woman, are in a trap, and your children are like butterflies in a glass jar. I can't say a thing that will bring you any comfort.

But you should tell your children exactly what you think and feel about the school: it is their only chance of escaping State indoctrination. To have mother on one's side is a great comfort.

I hate my lessons. Why do I have to study things like geography, history, math, and English? Will these studies do me any good?

This question comes from Sonia, age 14, Cleveland, Ohio. If I were a nice respectable headmaster, I'd say: "Sonia, my dear girl, you are too young to know what is good for you. We teach you these subjects so that you will be an educated woman when you grow up. These studies help you to reason, especially math. History shows you what has happened in the past, and becomes a guide later on when you are faced with difficult situations."

But, not being a nice headmaster, Sonia, I echo your question and ask what earthly good are these studies to anyone who doesn't of his own free will seek the knowledge. Years ago, in college, I got a grade of 95% in history. If anyone today asked me about some of the simplest facts in British history, I wouldn't be able to answer the questions. Why? Because I never was interested in British history. What good did all that study do me? The time spent in cramming useless facts robbed me of precious hours far better spent in doing the things I then liked.

Sonia, unless you become a teacher or a scientist, you will never do a simple equation in your life. Unless you do a very particularized sort of work, you will never remember the exports of Cambodia, and you will never want to know —after your exam—what they are.

Possibly one of the few things you will remember about American history will be that George Washington couldn't tell a lie; you won't be told that some of his presidential successors couldn't tell the truth.

Most subjects in school are a pure waste of youth's valuable time. I'd like to see schools made into creative places. But what can you and I do, Sonia? We are both in the same trap. I, too, have to teach certain subjects in my school because of the exam system. All boys and girls today experience the pressurizing of schools; they all know that their future depends on getting a college degree.

One of my old pupils is now 19. His teacher says he is a born musician. He applied to a London academy of music. He was rejected: he had not passed the standard examinations. Soon a Picasso will fail to enter an art school.

I get many a doleful letter from American school children. "Can I come to Summerhill? I hate my school; I hate the dull lessons, and the standardized teaching that kills any attempt to think with originality." Some add: "My teachers are sarcastic."

I can only say sadly: Face the beastly studies and look forward hopefully to the day you will leave school and begin your real education.

Why do you say that one of the necessary characteristics for a teacher is a sense of humor?

I don't know why; I just know that without humor you are a positive danger to children.

Humor to a child means friendliness, lack of respect and lack of fear; it means affection from the adult. School children are so unaccustomed to humor from teachers. When I say to a new boy of 10: "I'm looking for Neill. Do you know where he is?" he stares at me as if I were mad. I tried it on a girl of 11 who had been with us for three years. "Dunno," she said casually, "he went round that corner two minutes ago."

Humor, a priceless gift, is almost completely left out of a child's education. Tell a schoolboy that a polygon is a dead parrot, and he most likely will remember the term.

Small children have a sense of fun rather than a sense of humor. Ask a girl of 10 how many feet are in a yard. She will tell you. Then ask her how many feet there are in Scotland Yard and she may just stare at you. One of my pupils, accustomed to fun, immediately replied: "Depends on the number of cops and typists in the building."

Humor denotes equality. Humor is purposely kept out of the classroom because humor is a leveler. Humor would kill the respect the teacher demands because his laughter, mingling with that of his pupils, would make him too human.

I have had many a teacher who never criticized a child lest he become unpopular. He wound up not being popular. The pupils see through that pose, and despise the poseur. The moral is: You never can buy love.

The best teachers are those who laugh *with* their children; the worst are those who laugh *at* their children. We all know the nasty type of teacher who makes a class laugh at one of its members. Imagine how the scorned one feels.

I wonder why humor is suspect in so many walks of life. They say that the late Adlai Stevenson failed to become President of the United States because he was too prone to make jokes. I make the guess that every British Prime Minister studies his speeches most carefully to make sure he won't be accused of being a funny fellow.

When I was a journalist in Fleet Street, I was sent to interview George Robey, a comedian who had often made me laugh when I saw him on the stage. But when I met him off the stage, I found that in all my life I had never met such a solemn and pessimistic man. What a shock!

Which reminds me of the old story of the miserable man who went to see a psychiatrist about his pessimism. The doctor clapped him on the shoulder.

"You need cheering up," he said. "Go and see that great clown, Grimaldi."

"Ah!" sighed the patient. "I *am* Grimaldi!"

A teacher without humor is a danger, for humor is a

safety valve. If a man cannot laugh at himself, he is dead before his death. Someone once wrote that most men die when they are 40, but aren't buried until they are 70; he must have had in mind the humorless men.

There isn't a laugh in the Bible. Nor are there any laughs in school textbooks. Seeing Charlie Chaplin's *The Great Dictator* would be much more salutary for children than reading a history book on Hitler and Mussolini.

My friend's son wanted to drop out of college but his father would not allow it. Although his grades were poor, he managed to complete his college course. Today, that boy is a voluntary and eager student in a college of architecture which he couldn't have gotten into if he had dropped out and hadn't completed his undergraduate course. Today, that boy is grateful to his father for having forced him to stick to it. Isn't it true that sometimes a child can't judge what is good for him in the long run and has to be made to do things that he doesn't want to do?

A good question, indeed! What the sequel will be I cannot know, nor can anyone else at this stage. And the sequel is what counts.

Speaking generally, a boy who has to be forced to do something lacks the guts to make up his own mind. When he has no one—like a father—to tell him what to do, I query what initiative he will show in life.

In Summerhill, we never try to force anyone to study; if we did, the effect would be zero. This conclusion is based on a life-time of experience. But I can imagine cases where a kick in the pants would spur a boy onward, at least for the moment. Yet I must look far beyond the moment. I see a world full of people who were forced into professions and trades they did not choose for themselves. And that world is not a pretty one.

When I was 14, I was sent away 100 miles to be a clerk in a gas-meter factory. I failed at the job, and was then apprenticed to a draper. I hated both jobs. I was lucky to get out of them, but thousands of other men have to stick to a job they dislike all their lives. The world is filled with docile, resigned men and women who live their lives hating their work. But one should not dogmatize. The lad in question may be a success. If so, I would deem him an exception.

Of course, parents have to decide some things for their children—what school the child will go to, for instance. But if a parent, after choosing the school, says: "You must study Latin," he is going beyond his rights. The old time-honored cry "We are older and we know best" can be miserably wrong.

"*I suffered in life because I didn't study modern languages, and I insist on my kid's learning French and German.*" In such a statement how much parental concern is for the child's future, and how much can be charged to personal ambition?

Your question raises the whole complex of education. Children in school are forced, not only to attend class, but also to learn subjects they do not choose to study. Hence the Establishment, hence the vast majority of conditioned people who never challenge, hence the millions whose lives are dominated by their jobs. A father can force his son to complete his college course, but he cannot force him to be creative or to be happy or to be balanced. History tells of famous pianists who were forced as children to play for hours, but I wonder how many of these musicians turned out to be really happy human beings.

When a father compels his son to tread a certain path, he exercises force. But we should distinguish between force and advice, between pressure and suggestion. A few weeks ago, I had a young American visitor who said he wanted to become a teacher but who feared he was going to flunk his college courses becauses they were so dull. He asked my advice. I said: "I don't give advice; all I do is to set before you the alternatives. You say you want to teach children. Okay, but nobody will let you become a teacher of children, unless you have official qualifications—so it is up to you, chum." That speech was not forcing; it was simply commonsense which the listener might either accept or reject.

Coming back to the young architect: Was the lad brought up strictly so that he experienced unconscious rebellion against his father? Did fear make the lad obey his father's order to continue studying? Had the boy an ambition to be something non-academic: an artist, a musician, or an actor?

Yes, yes, I am willing to grant that in this case that kick in the pants worked; but I prefer a situation in which *the boy* knows what he wants in life, and realizing what his goal is, then wades through the school dung heap to go on to smell the roses.

I have seen too much of the type that boasts of early discipline. "*My father beat me as a kid when I was wrong and I have always been grateful to him. He made me what I am.*" I have never had the moral courage to ask mildly, "And what exactly *are* you?"

My son is a bright high school student who says he is eager to go to college and medical school. However, he does not really apply himself to his school work. He just does enough to get by. If his grades continue to be just passing, he will never be able to make med school. How can we make him understand, without pressuring him, that what he is doing now will affect his future?

Something wrong here. Your son, you say, wants to go to college, but the fact is that his actions deny the wish. It looks to me as if his avowed wish to go to college is but a pose to please his parents. Or the pose may simply be: *I'd better do what the other fellows do.*

I've had students at Summerhill who went on to college and some even became professors; but in every such case, there was no outside pressure or suggestion. Those lads *knew* what they wanted, and they buckled down and tackled the necessary subjects. A wish to succeed must come from within.

I know a boy of 19—not one of my pupils—whose father is a doctor. The boy says he also wants to be a doctor. But he cannot concentrate on anatomy and physiology; his mind is on cars, and he would really like to run a garage. For four generations the family has had a tradition of medicine. I hope the boy fails his exams and opens his garage. For that's what he *really* wants.

If your son wants to become a doctor, he will study. Why should *you* worry? It's his life, and he will live it according to *his* character, *his* abilities, and *his* ambition.

In our sick, invidious society, middle-class parents too often have a phobia—"*If my son isn't a college graduate, he will sink in the social sphere, and wind up being a manual laborer. The least we want him to be is a white collar worker. We want him to make a success of life.*"

All too often in the measurement of the word "success," the factor of personal happiness is ignored. A balanced father will not care a button whether his son becomes a taxi-driver or a tycoon. What he will care about is: "Is my son a happy man? Is he a credit to the human race?" In any case, you can't do much about the boy now. Be wise enough to leave the lad alone.

I've never had a pupil who made good at college when his motive was only to please his parents. Often, I have had to say to a parent: "So long as you keep encouraging your son to pass the exams, he won't pass." Parents must trust their child, must trust their youngster's motivation, not try to vicariously live their own lives again in the so-called achievements of their offspring.

Your boy probably has vital interests. For all I know his great ambition may be to become a jazz trumpeter in a combo. Whatever the boy yearns for, it's something more important to him than medicine.

Sorry, parent, the only advice I have to offer is: Leave him alone.

You say that in Summerhill children are not compelled to attend classes. How can children who are not obliged to attend lessons compete against public school students who have been compelled to learn subjects?

I think the answer is clear. My pupils at Summerhill study voluntarily and therefore they study with zest. In contrast, millions of public school pupils are obliged to study even when they hate the subject. I took seven years to learn enough Latin to enter the university. One of my boys achieved the same standard of proficiency in Latin in 15 months. Why was this so? Because that boy *wanted* to know Latin; I didn't.

So many school subjects are dull and boring for those who don't want to study those particular subjects. How many of my readers—the high school graduates—can right now do a square root or solve a quadratic equation? How many know a thing about King Phillip's War which they studied when they were supposed to be learning American colonial history? How many of you readers care a fig about King Phillip's War?

However, the exam system is here, and it can't be sidestepped. Boys and girls in Summerhill know they must pass these exams if they want to go to college. When the time comes to study, they buckle down to the necessary arduous study—that is, those who want to go to college. Freedom gives children guts; unpressured children can face difficulties when they have to.

Isn't it possible for a teacher to use Summerhill principles in a regular public school?

In a public school, the main work is learning school subjects. Attendance at classes is compulsory; duffers at math are compelled to sit there and do their best. There has to be discipline and an absence of noise. But free children make a lot of noise. In a conventional school, everything is against the teacher—the buildings, the lack of space for real play, the marshalling—indeed, the whole system.

Any young teacher in a big school will find that it is impossible to appreciably depart from the school curriculum, or for that matter, from even the school traditions and customs. A teacher in the regular school system cannot use as much freedom as he might like to. True, he can be on the side of the child, he can dispense with punishment, he can mitigate some of the homework, he can be human, he can even be jolly. Yet, in the ordinary overcrowded classroom such a free-wheeling teacher may find himself in all sorts of difficulties.

One of our old boys became a teacher in a school in which there were many tough kids. He said to me: "I began with Summerhill ideas, but I had to drop them. If I were nice to a rough specimen, he took me for a softy, and then my classroom turned into bedlam." That young teacher was fighting the system. He had little chance to succeed. His principal wouldn't have stood for bedlam—nor for any argument that the bedlam was only a stage, and that after the bedlam expended itself in time, the class would settle down to real work.

The drawback about extending freedom in a big public school is not alone that the authorities do not believe in freedom, but that most parents do not believe in freedom! Too many mothers and fathers regard school as a place in which their erring offspring will be disciplined. Fifty years ago in a Scottish village school, I experienced this parental attitude. I was a young teacher and was reproached by a succession of angry parents. "I send my laddie to the schule to lairn lessons, no to play a' day!"

The granting of freedom is possible in Summerhill because that is the condition under which we accept boys and girls. Furthermore, so many of our parents believe in freedom for their children, and for that very reason select the school.

HOMEWORK

I am a teacher. If homework is so awful, how is it that some of my students ask for it?

I have no objection to homework when it is asked for by pupils. Of course not.

If one of my pupils asks me to give her a few geometrical problems to solve in the evening, I am happy about it. What I object to is the many hours' grind at night foisted on school children in subjects in which they have no intrinsic interest. The proof of the pudding is that in almost every school there would be rejoicing if homework were abolished.

My girl of 11 won't do her homework and is failing in school. If she is put in the same class next term, she is going to be very unhappy. Shall I push her to study or shall I let her fail?

Woman, you *cannot* push her.

She already knows the consequences and has made her choice. Your child is alive and shows a healthy criticism of the system by refusing to take part in it.

How can you as an individual remedy a situation in which your daughter is the victim of a barbarous system? What good did homework ever do anyone? Home study— forced on a child—is DEAD study. Such forced study wrenches the child away from her play hours. Homework is resented because it has no true place in your daughter's sense of living.

It occurs to me: Maybe your daughter is not much of a scholar. Maybe her natural interests do not gravitate towards study. Must you force your values and ambitions on her? Far better for her to be a happy human being without a college degree, than an unhappy neurotic girl fighting her inner drives and armed only with a college diploma.

Sex

SEX EDUCATION

How should one handle the sex question?

There are but two ways to handle the sex question. One is the moral or religious way: sex is sinful, wrong, dirty. The other way is to be realistic about it.

Sex instruction in a school must be a pale affair; the parents would never stand for a lesson that told of the emotional part of sex, or for a lecture that spoke plainly of the bliss of sexual intercourse. It is ordained that the school treat only the barest facts of physiology. Personally, if sex is to be taught in this listless manner, I don't see the point about teaching sex at all.

From the safety angle, a girl has only to learn that intercourse without contraceptives can lead to pregnancy; and both sexes should be told again and again that venereal disease is real and dangerous. In a good society there would be no need to have any sex instruction at all; the subject would arise freely and naturally before adolescence in the home rearing, and would be handled by the parents freely and naturally.

I do not think the adolescent should be told too much about the technique of love-making; one of the delights of sex is the discovery of those techniques.

Most children get their sex information from other children; most of the information obtained in this way is distorted, pornographic, and sadistic. As a result, far too many a honeymoon is an experience in rape, and far too many married women have had a horror of sex since their first night.

MASTURBATION

My little children have begun to indulge in genital play with each other and with the children next door. I have scolded and spanked them. How can I stop them?

All children have genital play at one time or another—usually with guilt because parents make sex play a sin because of the adults' own guilt about sex. How many impotent men and frigid women owe their misery to early punishment for sex play? Wise parents leave children be, and ignore sex play; wiser parents will smile and approve.

If children tickled each others noses, parents would smile. What is wrong about genital tickling? Why are the sex organs heinous? Sex is here to stay; sex gives pleasure. Such is the arrangement of Nature to insure the continuance of the human animal.

When sex play is approved of by parents, the child does not get fixated on this one source of pleasure. But the best way to make masturbation a guilty complex to be carried on into adulthood is to label masturbation as evil and dirty. A child who masturbates or who has sex play with parental approval has the best chance later on of becoming a good lover—a lover who exhibits tenderness and joy. The universal sex misery largely stems from parental anti-sex. If you do not believe that the sexual misery is with us, read the Kinsey reports, a revelation of hypocrisy.

Now and then, my boy of five indulges in masturbation. He has never been restrained by myself or by my husband. He has no sense of wrongdoing or shame. At times, to the embarrassment of myself and my husband, he may play with himself in front of company. How should this be handled?

Under similar circumstances, a psychologist friend of mine said to his boy of six: "Tommy, your mother and I like you to play with your wee-wee, but you shouldn't do it when strangers are around because they think it's wrong to play with your wee-wee. *We* don't. So play with your wee-wee as much as you like, and as often as you like when we are alone and there's no company around."

Maybe a boy of five would not have the sophistication to grasp this, but it should be tried.

My little daughter of four frequently indulges in genital play. I understand that this is quite usual for a boy, but isn't this abnormal for a girl?

Genital play is as common among little girls as it is among little boys, only it is not so easily noticed. Little girls sometimes rub themselves against the edge of a table, or get a sex sensation riding a rocking horse, or underneath the bedclothes they simply tickle the vagina.

A wise mother will never interfere.

NUDITY

My husband and I feel very strongly about the sanctity and

dignity of the human body. We do not feel that we have to hide our bodies behind clothes. We have made it a practice to walk around the house nude. Some of my friends tell me that bringing up a child in an atmosphere of nudity can arouse unfavorable sexual reactions. Do you think so? Do you see any harm in my boy of 11 and his sisters of two and nine seeing each other's nakedness?

Dear lady, why listen to your anti-life friends? They have sex complexes; to them sex is dirty and bad.

"Unfavorable sexual reactions!" What do your friends mean? What is unfavorable about sex? Ignore your neighbors, lady. Ignore the dead. Nudity in a home is excellent, natural.

Your children will avoid so much sick sex later on; it's inconceivable that any of them will become a Peeping Tom; they will have seen all there is to see. Unlike so many repressed adolescents, they will not laugh obscenely when a breast, a brassiere, a toilet bowl, or a woman's thigh is shown on the movie screen.

MASCULINITY AND FEMININITY

Do you find that by nature boys and girls have different interests?

I do. At one time I thought that interests were determined by custom and training. The girls washed up and made the beds while the boys were not expected to do anything in the house. That was the vogue when I was a boy. Boys tinkered with bicycles; girls never did. Girls sewed and knitted while their brothers played marbles. I thought that when both sexes had freedom these differences would disappear. I was wrong.

Summerhill boys mend bikes, tinker with their radio sets, make things in the workshop—guns, swords, boats, planes, boxes. Seldom have we a girl who enters the workshop; seldom a bigger boy who attends a sewing class. Both sexes will make pots in the pottery and beaten brass trays in the metal shop. There is nothing much to differentiate between them in lessons, yet I could count on one hand the number of girls who liked mathematics. A few like algebra, but most girls shy away from geometry.

Both sexes like dancing, painting, acting, communal games. Many boys construct tree huts; some girls do, too. Boys dig holes and connect them by underground passages; girls never do. Freedom does not alter the innate predilection of the sexes.

MENSTRUATION

When should I tell my daughter about periods?

A goodish time before they are due to start. I have known girls who got into a panic, and thought they were bleeding to death.

CIRCUMCISION

I am not Jewish, but many of my gentile friends have their infant sons circumcised. Should I follow their example?

Why? On medical grounds? Whatever its history may be, circumcision is a symbolic castration. The rite is meant to weaken a child's sex; the talk about prevention of veneral disease is pure rationalization.

Is there any evidence that the uncircumcised suffer more from venereal disease than the circumcised? Circumcision is a cruel and barbarous custom which no humane parents should tolerate. Savages mutilate their faces; some put rings through their nostrils; and we, the superior races, smile at their childishness. Are we less savage when we mutilate a baby's penis?

So, my dear questioner, I advise you not to be influenced by what the neighbors think, or for that matter, by what the specialists say. Any mutilation brings shame and inferiority. Men who lost an eye or a limb in war usually suffer from a great sense of embarrassment. As an extreme, imagine the feelings of a man in a nudist camp wearing a truss. Even dental plates are a source of shame to many people. I have more than once had a circumcised pupil who refused to undress in front of the other boys. I am convinced that unconsciously a young circumcised man may feel that he has lost something, been deprived of something very important.

No, do not do anything to your baby boy that will make him feel less of a man later on in life.

CONTRACEPTIVES

My teenage daughter wants to have a sex life. Should I fit her out with a diaphragm?

Dear lady, you can say no and then you'll have a head-ache every time she goes out with a boy friend. You'll be worried stiff about her getting pregnant. When she goes to a party you will be frightened lest she drink too much, and then tumble into bed with a boy who has also had too much to drink. True, this situation could happen even if you had her properly equipped, for she might not always carry her contraceptive with her.

You might let her have "the pill," but then would you be happy? It's your negative attitude—your fear of sex—that gives you so much concern. More important, your concern transmits itself to your daughter and gives her a sense of guilt. Not only is she frustrated by a dammed up sexual urge, but she is fighting all the time against your values which are at odds with hers.

Sex must go somewhere. If barred from its natural outlet, it may take the way of masturbation which is never altogether satisfying; natural sex means giving and receiving and tenderness. Or her sex may be sublimated, or at least seemingly so. Or the dam may break and the girl may suddenly find herself in a jam.

Compared with Sweden, America is far behind the times. In Sweden, it is no disgrace to have an illegitimate child, and the State in its allowances for mothers makes no difference between the married woman and the unmarried woman. I have the feeling that America lives in fear—fear of Communism, fear of sex, fear of low status, fear of a poor income, and worst of all—fear that the young will challenge the opinions and wishes of the old.

The family in the U.S.A. can be a most dangerous com-pulsive institution—and not only the family that indoctri-nates with religion—but also the family that is liberal, that takes part in demonstrations against the war in Vietnam, that battles against color prejudice, and against out-of-date divorce laws. Not seldom does such a family have the same repressive attitude to the children as the most conservative family. These "liberal" parents also want to guide their children: *We are older than you, and wiser than you, and we know best what is good for you.*

I disagree. These parents don't know what is good for their children. That is why so many seemingly fine homes lose their children and never find them again.

If I were you I should certainly take my daughter to a doctor to be given full contraceptive advice.

On the other hand, I have more than once seen a mother try to force a sex life on her daughter. I have heard a 16-year-old girl cry: "Mother, I tell you I don't want a sex life yet." Such mothers are usually women who compensate for their previously inhibitive treatment by offering a conscience-saving sexual freedom, a freedom often not accepted because of the prior maternal teachings. Such mothers do wrong to pressure their daughters. *Sex shouldn't be handled by pressure, either for or against.* Sex is highly personal; no individual should dictate to another sexual timing or sexual response.

A girl of 20 said to her mother: "In my set, every girl seems to sleep with a fellow; the girls tease me because I don't want to. I begin to feel that I should because I feel I don't fit in."

Here we have group pressure—a sad situation. It brings up the question of promiscuous sex, sex without love or tenderness. But we must try not to be moral about it. A young couple can have sex together with much pleasure, even though they are not in love with each other. But the young man or young woman who goes on looking for casual chances for intercourse must have a sex life that lacks something of value, call that something love or tenderness, call it what you will. There can be no permanent pleasure in promiscuity. Girls realize this when they talk about "having a steady," partly of course, because a steady supposes likely marriage. The happiest love affairs I have seen were those which had some permanancy. The Cassanovas and the Don Juans are not likely to give a girl anything like full enjoyment.

To return to your question: a girl or a boy should be free to have a sex life when she or he wants it. Without parental approval, such a sex life will be apt to be a guilty one; without contraceptives, a dangerous one.

HOMOSEXUALITY

Do you think homosexuality wrong or a sin?

Of course, homosexuality is not a sin. A person cannot control his innate likes and dislikes. One can control behavior, but not feelings. The law is barbaric when it sends a deviate to prison.

Would I appoint a homosexual or a Lesbian to a position on my school staff? No. But that is not saying that homosexuality is wrong; it is only saying that it is inconvenient. For in the present state of society the homosexual is a pariah —he has to hide his nature. Because of society's attitude, he is seldom happy. He has to keep his sex life secret and devious, and he constantly risks blackmail.

We are all bisexual; we are all part man and part woman. Heterosexuality is the norm, the biological basis of life. But no one with a healthy attitude to sex will condemn the homosexual or be shocked by homosexuality. Surely, private homosexual activity can harm no one not directly involved; so why all the fuss and feathers and the criminal proceedings against consenting adults.

We have crying evils: our insane divorce laws, our cruel laws against homosexuals, our laws against abortion (in spite of the fact that there are thousands of illegal and dangerous abortions every year.) But for a legislator to vote for a humane law about abortion might result in the loss of the Catholic vote or the Baptist vote or the what not vote. That is why crying evils take at least three generations to be abolished by law.

My son, William, now 17, pals around with a group of boys who somehow misimpress me. Some of them seem effeminate. I haven't any direct evidence of homosexuality or misbehavior of any sort, but I am in great fear that my son may be lured into becoming a homosexual. There's so much of it in this country now. Is there any way in which I can detect such a tendency in the boy? And, if so, is there anything that we can do about it?

You can't do anything about it by talking or advising. Every one of us has a homosexual potential, and too many situations go to develop that component—worst of all, our segregated schools. Sex must go somewhere; too often, homosexual relationships are formed under conditions of sexual segregation. But homosexuality can develop, too, in a so-called co-ed school, where boys and girls mix only in classes. Real co-education is, to me, the ideal way to counteract homosexuality.

No one definitely knows what causes a man to become a homo, or causes a woman to become a Lesbian. A common theory is that the boy has an unsatisfactory father, and is forced to channel too much love to his mother; then the incest factor makes the mother taboo, and that taboo carries over indiscriminately to all women. But I have often noticed that a homo, who has no use for girls, is most attentive and tender with older women.

No parent has the power to abolish those situations that tend to encourage the homosexual element: armies, segregated schools, prisons.

When you complain about your son's living largely in a gang of youths, I am compelled to guess that your boy feels estranged from you and that he is rebelling against your authority. Most homos of both sexes, I daresay, come from unhappy homes. At this juncture, I am sorry to say you can do little about your son's incipient homosexuality. Psychotherapy may help the boy to stave off what you fear.

Influencing Children

Is the parent always at fault? Is every problem child the product of wrong handling?

Certainly most such cases would appear to be the result of a bad home, yet we get some children who apparently came from good homes who are disturbed. I have no idea why, for example, two twin boys should turn out so differently. Tom is social and sincere, while Bill is a young sadist. That is why I often say that psychology is at the Stone Age.

I have seen the seven-year-old son of intelligent, modern parents look like a Gestapo torturer, his face hard, his eyes cruel. He looked as if he had no pity—worse, he looked like he would never learn pity. That boy loved to torture animals. His parents had given him love, and as much freedom as their environment allowed. The sad fact is that, even if we knew the causes, we could do little or nothing in such a case. An unnoticed injury at birth, an early fall, nonfunctioning glands—any of these could be the cause.

I know of no treatment to touch sources of this kind. When I began Summerhill, I imagined that psychology would cure anything and everything. I took pupils with birth injuries, pupils with sleeping sickness, pupils who walked backwards. I could do nothing with them. If others have succeeded with these types, I should joy to hear how they did it.

Take the case of a child who was unwanted, one whose birth had followed an unsuccessful attempt at abortion. If such a child has a hate attitude to life, what can we do

about it? I might appear here to be handing parents a sop—
We have a bad boy, and it isn't our fault. Alas, in the great
majority of cases, the parents *are* at fault. Possibly the
worst parents are those who cry: "We have done everything
for that kid, and he is a boor and a heartbreak." Not all,
but a great many problem children suffer from the repres-
sions, buried hates, and frustrations of their parents.

**I am pregnant with my first child. I have read what you said
in SUMMERHILL about fears of the expectant mother being
transmitted to the child in the uterus. But all this is unconscious, is it not? What can I do, being the kind of person I
am, not to transmit fear to my unborn child when I am
aware that I suffer from great anxieties?**

But I only said, if I remember aright, that it may be
that when a woman does not want to have a child, her unconscious worry may have an affect on the child and make
the babe fear life from the start. I have no proof of the
validity of this theory; it may be all wrong.

Every woman and every man suffers from anxiety in
some form. A woman who does not want to give birth to
her child may hate the father; she may fear losing her figure. If the child is to be illegitimate, she may fear public
opinion, and try in vain to have an abortion. I imagine that
if a pregnant woman fears flying, her fear would not affect
the child in the womb. I don't know; nobody knows. And it
is only my guess that fear of the birth itself can give the
baby a feeling of anti-life from the moment of birth on. If
you, dear lady, want to have your baby, there is no cause
for concern.

I am sorry if I made you worry. But cheer up; at least, you are conscious of your anxieties. It is the buried anxieties that are very likely the most dangerous.

Our daughter is 21. She is off in Paris studying art. She has been there for two years now, and she just doesn't want to come home. My husband sends her a weekly allowance on which she lives. We visited her recently, and we found her to be seriously engaged in studying art, quite happy, and utterly horrified about our insistence that she has had enough time abroad and should come back to the States. My husband feels that she is entitled to live her own life, but by the same token she dare not ask us to support her financially in the life she has chosen to lead. I know that if my husband cuts off her allowance, she will live in a garret, so to speak, take a menial job, and support herself. I tremble to think of my little girl living under such harsh conditions, and I resist my husband's suggestion. He says that our daughter must now grow up and face the music. I shudder to think what will happen to her. Who is right—my husband or I?

I think your husband is wrong. If the lassie is happy in Paris why is your husband not content, even delighted? Or is his love possessive? It is not clear whether he grudges the money or whether he thinks that the girl has no right to happiness—unless she is happy under *his* conditions.

And why does she not want to go home anyway? Her life in Paris may be so absorbing that to return to a suburban, conventional environment would be hell for her. Her refusal may be a protest against a father who may have exercised his authority with her all her life.

Money is often a substitute for love. There is many an unloved child who gets far too expensive presents from his parents. In this case, if money means love, the father is withdrawing his love from her. If the father were a comparatively poor man, he might well ask the daughter to support herself, but I have a feeling that in this case the father has the means to support her.

Let's review the situation. Mr. X has a daughter who is happy in France. He is a conventional American with a regard for status symbols. He wants to have his daughter home to look well in the family Cadillac, to entertain his business friends, to take part in his usual social rounds. "If my girl stays away too long," he conjectures, "my friends will begin to think that there is something wrong with her home. In France, she may pick up some artist guy, with long hair and a beard and no money. But I want her to marry a young executive and maintain a position in life with all the good things that money can buy."

Your husband should ask himself: "Do I love my daughter or do I not? If I do, then I'll give her an allowance as long as she needs it. If I love her, I'll leave her free to choose any kind of life or any kind of mate she wants to. I won't pressure her to live *my* kind of life."

CAREER

I have built up a good business, and naturally, I want my sons to carry it on when I am gone. One boy wants to go on the stage, and the other wants to be an airman. What can I do?

Nothing, absolutely nothing! Sixty years ago, your boys would have done what Dad told them to do, and would have gone into the business. Having no heart in it, they would possibly have ruined it.

After all, what has the business to offer them? Financial security, but at the probable expense of mental stagnation.

Your sons want to do something active. On the other hand, you seek security for them. It is a simple matter of preference: a big house in White Plains with three cars and a social round of inanities—or a world of adventure in the studio or in the air.

Yet it is not so simple after all. A man works hard to build up a good business. He made it, it is his child, he is possessive about it. To think of his creation dying with him is a bitter thought. I can understand how you feel. I built up Summerhill; I think it a wonderful place. But if my heirs want to turn it into a horseriding academy, the idea does not trouble me, for I'll be gone and I won't be able to suffer disappointment. The case here is different. You are alive; you see your sons abandoning your lifework. You probably enjoyed years of happiness building up your business, proving that it is better to travel hopefully than to arrive.

But if your sons seek another road to happiness—you, Father, may sigh, but you should just reach for the whisky bottle, grin into the glass, and say: "*I* did what I wanted to. They have the same privilege."

In fact, each of your boys may achieve more in his way than you did in yours. Many sons go into business and live little, unadventurous lives. For what? Security, respectability, the status of the little man? One should rejoice when the young leave the trodden path, and go out seeking the life abundant.

My wife and I are musicians, devoting our lives to music.
Our son is eight, old enough in my opinion to study the violin. He hasn't asked for lessons. Every time I approach the
subject he puts me off. I know that if he is going to become
a good musician, he will have to start early. Is it right for me
to pressure him into music lessons? I feel he isn't old enough
to know what's good for him.

But, Father do *you* know what's good for him? Music
may mean nothing to him. It would be a crime if you
forced him to play the fiddle against his inclination.

You have accepted the fallacy that because music is a
joy for you, it should be and will be a joy for your son. "Oh
Ho!" say I, "Not so easy!" Christen a boy Beethoven Mozart
Jones—and he may turn out to be a boxer.

We have no right to fashion a child's life. I have heard
the argument ad nauseum for years: *"The child does not
know enough; if I don't teach him music or art or poetry,
he may feel the lack of it in after years."* Rubbish! If the
boy is a born Bach nothing will keep him from music.

Why the fallacious argument is usually about music I
don't know. I never hear a parent say: "We must force our
son to learn biology, so that later on in life he shouldn't
blame us for his ignorance about this subject."

I used to teach in a London school where the concert-
ist, Solomon, was a pupil. At seven, no one could have kept
him from the piano. What would have become of him had
his parents insisted that he become an astronomer?

It is all wrong—this parental molding of a child's interests. I have a shrewd suspicion that this young lad has
heard so much piano and violin that he would like to live
in a silent world.

Father, if you force your boy to study the violin you may live to regret it.

CENSORSHIP

Should I censor my daughter's reading? She is 15 and she brings home books that to me are objectionable.

If you want her to acquire a good taste in pornography, certainly ban her books. I recall the day when my parents forbade the reading of Hardy's *Tess of the D'Urbervilles*. We all devoured it in secret.

Censorship is plain silliness. If Mary does not know a popular four-letter word and she sees that word in a book, it will mean nothing to her. If she already knows that word, reading it won't corrupt her.

Censorship denotes fear of sex and nothing else. When a home is free about sex, no book nor film is dangerous. Censorship is an extension of parental lying, the old traditions that lied about Santa Claus, and about madness following masturbation. Censorship may have worked to some extent in Victorian days, but censorship does not work today. Youth is all the better for its freedom to decide for itself what is good and what is bad. How slowly things do move! Some parents are but little in advance of the Victorian ladies who clothed the legs of a grand piano. There's a campaign in the U.S. now to force pet owners to make their pets modest by clothing them in trousers! This seems to me to be so inane that I'm tempted to regard it as the joke of some sarcastic wag.

My school library in Summerhill contains *Lady Chatter-*

ley's Lover, The Tropic of Cancer, Fanny Hill; I never see my adolescents reading them. The law makes the crime, and censorship makes pornography. And pornography continues to nourish the sickness of humanity.

My kids are crazy about comics. I have read that comics are not good for children. However, in my home I have not seen any bad results from the reading of comics. What do you think?

When I was a boy, comics were comical. Today, many comics are horrible: pictures of eyes being gouged out or scenes of half-naked women being beaten with whips. Though we may abominate magazines that show sadism and perversion, *censorship* of the comic is far worse than the comic itself.

As adults, how many of us are free from interest in the same type of picture? We watch Cassius Clay on TV beat and beat a tottering Patterson. We have a prurient interest in sex scenes which imply lascivious doings.

You cannot keep all accounts of violence from children. Your daily newspaper tells that a white man wantonly murdered a black man. Bad enough! But then the paper goes on to say that the Southern jury brought in a verdict of *Not Guilty.* Here is murder crowned with injustice. Yet you do not bar that newspaper from your children.

You can't screen the young from the evils of the day— you can only live in a way that will make such evils appear to them to be unattractive. I said *live*—not preach!

UNDESIRABLE COMPANIONS

My son has become friendly with a boy who doesn't have a very nice character—he is a liar, a bully, a swaggerer. My son is beginning to imitate his ways. How can I make my son realize that this boy is a bad influence on him?

Every boy comes across companions who are bullies and liars and swaggerers. The balanced boy soon comes to realize the posings and inferiority of the lying boaster. You cannot help matters by trying with words to wean the boy from his unsatisfactory companion.

I think the best, the only way, is to make your son's life as full and happy as you can. Ask yourself if he is seeking this other boy because his home is too good, too moral, too restricted. He must be attracted to the companion because from him he gets something that he cannot get at home.

But why worry so much about lying and swaggering? Most folks, old and young, do their bit of both even when they aren't politicians and sales agents. If your boy lies to you, he most likely is afraid to tell you the truth for fear you'll jump on him.

People do not go on imitating others, unless the faults of the imitated are what they consciously or unconsciously would like to have. The hero attracts those who want to be like him. Hitler's SS attracted all the sadists and perverts in Germany. Billy Graham attracts all the simple who believe they are sinners. You do not follow a leader unless he is going the way you want to go. I really feel there may be something lacking in your home.

RELIGION

Is it fair to keep children from knowing about God?

Which God do you mean? The one who makes masturbation a sin, or the one who created the universe?

I could tolerate Christianity if its adherents lived up to
their religion and turned the other cheek, sold all they had,
and gave the proceeds to the poor. I could admire the
Church if the Vatican and Canterbury symbolized the
poverty life of Jesus, instead of parading golden candle-
sticks and golden images and ornate vestments.

According to the believers, Bertrand Russell will roast
forever in hell, while Billy Graham will sit at the right hand
of God. Punishment without let-up is to be the doom of a
man who has enriched mankind with his creative mathematics. Such is the unfeeling God the young are supposed
to believe in—a God who is cruel and unremittingly tor-
tures a good man who never harmed anyone but who just
didn't pronounce the proper mumbo-jumbo.

Speaking of Billy with his cry that salvation is only
through Jesus Christ, what does he think will be the fate of
the vast majority of humanity who through no fault of
theirs never heard of Jesus Christ?

Jesus gave out much love and charity and understanding. But among his followers were John Calvin who had
his rival Servetus roasted over a slow fire, St. Paul who
hated women, and the Calvinist Church of South Africa
which supports apartheid.

I understand that in some parts of the United States
a teacher is unlikely to be appointed if he avows he has no
religion. Unless he believes in a certain mythology, he is

unfit to teach geometry.

In today's newspaper, there is a report of a young woman who on her application blank for the position of nurse in a hospital said she was a Free Thinker. She was rejected because the authorities of that institution held that only Christians are capable of showing a patient love. So much of organized religion today is hypocritical and holier-than-thou. How can Christ's followers be so anti-life when they pretend to be disciples of the preacher who asked if any man was pure enough to cast the first stone at a woman of easy virtue.

I once took on a Catholic boy against my better judgment. The experiment failed. The boy was brought into a school that does not believe in sin or punishment; then he had to go to a priest and confess his sins. The poor lad simply did not know where he stood.

At a recent lecture one questioner asked: "You are a Humanist. Why don't you teach Humanism?" I replied that it is as bad to teach Humanism as it is to teach Christianity. I do not believe that children should be molded in any way nor converted to any belief.

Take the Humanists who challenge belief in a God. I know Humanists who are just as anti-sex as Christians are; I know Socialists who are just as moral as the deepest dyed Col. Blimp. I know Communists who worship their Marxian gods as emotionally and unthinkingly as any Catholic worships his Holy Mother.

If there is such a thing as sin, it is the propensity of adults to tell the young how to live—a preposterous impulse seeing that adults themselves do not know how to live.

No one should try to educate the emotions; one can only create an environment in which the emotions can be fully expressed. If the emotions are free, the intellect will look after itself.

To answer your question specifically. It is neither fair nor unfair to expose or not to expose a child to religion. A child will absorb the values of his parents whether theology is present or absent and whether the values are pro-life or anti-life.

Knowing about God isn't nearly as important as intimate knowledge of well-behaving, loving parents who are honest with themselves and with everyone else.

Our family has been Presbyterian for generations, and we take pride in our church affiliation. My son, James, is completely uninterested in church attendance. We are enormously embarrassed when our friends ask us on Sundays where James is. Do you think it would be an imposition for us to insist that James cater to some extent to our feelings? Is it too much to ask a boy to give up an hour a week for something that his parents feel so deeply about?

It looks as if you are more concerned about what the neighbors think than about the spiritual welfare of James. He says that church bores him—then what point is there in forcing him to go? If he has a spark of religion left in him, this compulsion would be likely to quench it forever.

There are very many Jameses in the modern world; thousands of young people are taken to church against their will. We cannot make anyone believe by using force, or suggestion, or what not. James, like many young people born into our scientific world, may be an agnostic or an atheist; he may even be sensitive enough to ask why Christianity has so little to do with Christ and his teachings of brotherly love, or he may well ask how is it that so many religious parents beat and browbeat their boys. James may take literally the command: "Suffer little children to come unto me."

Or if he has no special views, James may find the sermons dull; the hymns, banal and unmusical. After all, what boy other than a child indoctrinated from the cradle on, would prefer church-going over TV or the movies or just plain play.

No, you have no right whatsoever to force James to do something he does not want to do. In your own interests, you must realize that forcing is a good way to lose James' love.

All the kids on our block go to Sunday School. My husband and I do not believe in organized religion. John asks why he can't go to Sunday School with his playmates. As staunch believers in the balefulness of religious training, how can we handle this situation?

Your boy isn't seeking *religion;* he is simply wanting to be part of his gang, to do what his mates do. If his pals went every Sunday to a KKK school, he would want to join them.

If you say no, you may give him a life interest in religion. Forbidden fruit tastes sweet. I advise you to let him go. And if he begins to think of himself as a miserable sinner, *then* tell him what you think of religion. Remember that the home has a deeper influence than any school.

I grant that agnostics and Humanists are up against an entrenched majority. Our TV and radio give much time to the religionists and seldom even ten minutes to the Humanists.

But let your boy go to Sunday School if he wants to. If your home is a happy one, your son won't be likely to seek any form of religion. My 60 happy pupils never betray any interest in the subject.

Summerhill sounds like heaven, but why, oh why, do you not teach religion?

In my school, we do not teach religion because we live it, that is if being religious means to give out love.

It isn't what one believes that matters, it is what one *is* and what one *does*. Some parsons hunt the fox; some shoot partridges. Many a religious parent beats his child. No matter what such a parent proclaims, his hateful action proves his religion of love is a sham. How many children have been beaten for not having learned a page from the Shorter Catechism.

But enough. If the word God means *good*, then this God we certainly try to follow in Summerhill.

CHARACTER MOLDING

I am a pacifist. Should I try to make my children pacifists?

Humanity can be divided into two classes: those who have accepted Father and have thus become members of the Establishment, and those who have rejected Father and have become rebels. The former make up the great majority.

In the upper classes, many lads challenge the Father Philosophy at 20; at 50, they vote Tory.

A father can be a pacifist and at the same time an unsatisfactory father. He may be a fuss-pot; he may be moral about sex; he may have a religion that does not appeal to youth. In a pacifist home as well as in any other kind of home, there may be children who protest against the subtle molding.

No, I don't think you should make a conscious effort to convert your family to your way of thinking. If the home has a love basis, your sons and daughters will unconsciously be influenced by your ideas, and the chances are that your children will accept pacifism.

My friend, I don't think anyone should attempt to form his child's life or thoughts. We must be ready to accept behavior from our offspring—and beliefs, too—that go against our grain. One pacifist father I knew had a son who was mad about flying. The only way to learn flying was to join the local flying corps training school. The father sternly forbade his entering a military establishment. The son ran away and joined the R.A.F. That father should have bowed to his son's wishes.

We must not try to live our children's lives for them. I am a Humanist, but I would not dare to try to convert my child to Humanism or to any other creed or conviction. I will answer my daughter's queries, but I wouldn't think of beginning a campaign to get her to think in the way I do. She sees the way I live. If she approves of that way, she may follow it. But nothing I could ever *say* would be more eloquent or meaningful than my behavior has been.

The same observation applies to convictions. My child by this time should know what I believe in. No need to convince her one way or the other. She's had ample time by observance to find out whether she agrees or disagrees.

No, live and let live, I say.

I discount so much appearing in psychoanalytical literature about hidden motives . . . . the pacifist is a sadist over-compensating for his unconscious cruelty, or the pacifist is a physical coward rationalizing his motives to avoid being killed in battle. One might just as well say that the torturing Gestapo was over-compensating for a strong unconscious love for the Jews. And if all this attributing of thought and action to unconscious motives is right, one would think that psychoanalysts themselves, having discovered their own unconscious drives, would be wonderful men free from all complexes. Having met dozens of them in my time, I can assure you that analysts don't behave much different from most other people.

My wife and I are active in furthering civil rights. We are dead against the war in Vietnam. Our children, a boy of 18 and a girl of 16, have no desire to take part in civil rights marches. They won't even wear an anti-bomb badge. We are disappointed in them. Should we try to get them to follow in our footsteps to a freer world?

Certainly not! Anyway, you couldn't if you tried.

You should not expect your children to be replicas of yourselves. They are possibly fed up with the whole she-bang, for in your home there must be so much talk about your beliefs and your actions. Maybe those kids of yours are so busy protesting against their home pressures, they have no energy left to protest against the treatment of Negroes.

A "liberal" home is not always a *liberal* home. You can't convert anyone by talking or by preaching. Oh, yes, a Billy Graham can convert a mass of people whose emotions have been dammed up for years, but, in most cases, how long such a conversion lasts is questionable. *Parents should not try to convert their children to anything!*

The opposite holds true, too. I have just answered a school girl in Chicago. I wrote, "Don't try to convert your parents to a belief in Summerhill. You say they are against it. Anything you say to them will not alter their belief one iota." There are cases of true conversion, but only when the convert has been unconsciously seeking conversion for some time.

Your children reject your philosophy of life. Leave it at that; you have no control. Even if your boy became a member of the Klu Klux Klan, or if your girl went out on the streets, you could do nothing about it. I make the guess that the two of them feel they've had enough indoctrination at home to last a lifetime.

It is perhaps easier to indoctrinate hate than love. All those white children in the deep South I see on TV have faces full of hate when they stone Negro children. That hate is not natural; it was forced on them all the way from babyhood. Hate seems to breed hate more easily than love breeds love, hence the sickness of humanity. To have a hating parent must be one of the worst handicaps a child can ever have.

Again, I say to you parents: leave your children alone. If it is really in them, they will find their own way to protest against all that is ugly and hateful in life. If they truly believe the downtrodden should be succored, they will find their own way to help. If they are impervious to others' needs, nothing you might say will make one whit of difference.

A youth of 17 said to me: "I march in the anti-bomb marches in London and all the time I keep thinking of their futility, for I know that our minority has absolutely no power to alter the policy of the men who rule us." Right, or wrong, he has a point.

Free children are not propagandizing rebels; they often wear anti-nuclear badges, but none was arrested for sitting down with Bertrand Russell in Trafalgar Square. Indeed, I think I am the only Summerhillian who was tried for sitting down as a protest. I sat down in Scotland at the Polaris Base, and got 60 days or a fine of £10. I didn't try again because I concluded that it was a method that cut little or no ice.

No, freedom does not make rebels. And here an awkward question arises: To rebel against the Establishment, must one have first suffered bitterly from it? As Shelley puts it:

> *Most wretched men are cradled into poetry*
> > *through wrong;*
> *They learn in suffering what they teach in song.*

Coming back to your question: Parents must try to see the point of view of their children. It could be that your youngsters feel deeply about the matters that concern you, but also feel—though they won't express it—that pragmatically, you're all wet in your approach.

In my teaching, I have never intruded my own personal problems, so that if you ask any of my pupils questions about my personal life they would not know the answer. What are my politics, my attitude to religion, to doctors and to drugs? They would not know. Happily they would not care.

The greatest danger is for a teacher to impress his pupils with his own creeds. The business of teaching is to stimulate thinking—not to implant beliefs.

Suppose a man seriously believed that the earth is flat, and he spent his leisure marching along with a huge banner to proclaim his truth—I can hardly imagine that any son would be likely to march with him. Would you deem such a boy disrespectful or ungrateful? Your beliefs and your passions are your own: don't foist them on your children.

How can I imbue my children with an attitude of love and reverence for life when all about them they experience hatred and prejudice and hostility and war?

This is a poser. How *can* you?

Yet we manage to do it in Summerhill. Our ex-pupils will never be haters of Negroes or Jews, nor will they be warmongers. Our kids grow up to be charitable and tolerant, but certainly not ignorant of the sick world they live in. Give a child a happy home and a happy school and the risk of his becoming a hater will be small, indeed.

At Summerhill, we have many small children. We have cats and hens and geese that wander about the children's paths with no fear at all; indeed, it is sometimes hard to get the cackling geese to move out of the way. Give children love and freedom and they will automatically have a reverence for life, both animal and human, I know of no other way.

Our reform schools for delinquents with their strict

discipline and punishment breed hatred all the time. Every spanking father makes his child hate and fear. Every stupid roaring teacher has the same effect. The only hope for this sick world is a new generation of children who are allowed to love life and not to hate it.

But, alas, the vast majority of children are damned from the beginning—damned by discipline, by preachings, by punishment, damned by indoctrination by people who, in their time, were led to hate life.

So when I go to a teachers conference and listen to speeches about exams and careers, I just feel sick. The only good education in home or in school is one that allows the emotions to be free.

MARRIAGE

We are Jewish and our son wants to marry a gentile. Should we forbid the marriage?

I do not know if you are orthodox or not. You may never go to synagogue, yet retain the traditions of your religion and your family. Yet I hope you will permit your son to marry his gentile love. I hope so for your sake, as well as for your son's sake.

I once knew a famous Jewish artist who had to "live in sin" with his beloved and did not marry her until his parents died. It all seemed so daft, so stupid, so narrow. Yet it is not only religion that seeks to control love; social class exercises much the same pressures for Park Lane does not seek its brides in Whitechapel. In real life, a merchant prince rarely marries a Cinderella.

Parents, forbid the match and lose your son's trust and love. Do you want it on your conscience that you have stopped him from marrying someone he loves? How will you feel if he drops this girl, and then goes on to marry an acceptable Jewess who leads him a hellish life? Of course, this may not happen—but then again, it may. And if it does, he'll always be thinking: "*My father and mother got me into this mess, and wrecked my life.*"

Parents are so many times inclined to judge a potential marriage by externals. "*She plays the piano so nicely, and her father is a highly respected and successful doctor.*" "*He graduated with an M.A., and his father's a Superintendent of Schools.*" As if playing the piano or having a successful father insures compatibility and happiness.

Parents, too, see things in a biased manner, depending on whether they are regarding their child or their child-in-law. There's the illuminating story about a visitor who asks her neighbor, "Mrs. Rosenberg, how is your daughter Shirley?"

"Oh, Shirley?" comes the answer, "She has such a wonderful husband. A mink coat, a Cadillac, servants galore! Such a fine husband! He serves her her breakfast in bed, and she doesn't ever get up till noon. Such a prince!"

"And your son, Sam?"

"Sam? What a bitch *he* married! He bought her a fur coat, and a car, and gives her every luxury. But she stays in bed till noon! Won't even get up to give him his breakfast!"

What is your opinion of mixed marriage?

I think I should be a little concerned—not about the

wedding—but about the children, for in our society a half caste must feel inferior. But I myself move in a society where no one cares whether a girl is a mulatto. So with anti-Semitism; we have Jewish children in Summerhill, and no one cares; most of our children don't even know who is Jewish.

My daughter is 16. She is head over heels in love with a young man of 20 who attends college. The boy wants to marry her, and she is pressing me to allow it. This young man has wealthy parents who are willing to support him through college and somewhat thereafter, so there isn't an economic roadblock here. However, I feel that 16 is too young an age for marriage. My daughter is as mature as anyone is at her age, but I just can't get over my conviction that she is simply too young to get married. What do you think?

I personally would let her marry the man, but I can see your maternal worry clearly. The girl is ready for a sex life and wants one. The marriage might end in failure, but that might happen if she were 26.

Let me indulge in fantasy. The youth is called up in the draft. He dies a miserable death in Vietnam. The girl cries: "We could have had, at least, a short time of happiness. They wouldn't let me live with love."

But, mother, I also sympathize with you. The young man has money, and you may imagine your daughter's being swept into the rat race and its inanities with all that the young man's wealth can provide—the expensive clothes, the big car, the mad social round. Your daughter may be being offered a surface world, with everything deep and important shoved aside.

What is the alternative? A feeling on the part of your daughter that if she were loved by you, you would not frustrate her young love. You might really ask her to wait for a year; but if you demand that the waiting period be sexless, your daughter will still have a grouse.

It is so dangerous for parents to interfere with love. I have known more than one case where the parents thought the match unsuitable—lower class, you know—and they stopped the wedding. Then the girl, on the rebound, married the wrong man and misery.

You will have to weigh up the consequences of your decision with as much detachment as you can. Your question omits such important factors as: Do you personally like the youth? Do you think he is balanced enough to be a husband? Is your own sex life satisfactory; and if not, have your anxieties roots in your own fear? Are you frightened about almost everything? Is your daughter unhappy at home and seeking the first opportunity to leave it?

Another point. Doctors agree that girls reach maturity a good deal earlier than they did a generation ago. This girl may, at 16, be as ready for marriage as the 21-year-old of yesterday.

And, mother, bear in mind that many a girl has run away from home when faced with a ban on her love affair. If this happened, you would have a much greater worry on your mind.

Problems of Childhood

My husband and I disagree about what to do with our six-month-old little girl when she cries. I want to pick her up and comfort her. My husband says I will turn her into a spoiled, demanding child. What do you think?

I think you are right and your husband is wrong. No child cries for nothing. The baby may be in pain, or lonely, or hungry; most likely she cries because she wants to be loved.

I wonder how much of the sickness of humanity is due to the ignorance of what a baby needs. No child is ever spoiled by having too much love. Your husband's way will give her emotional starvation and fears, possibly a neurosis for life. Please understand: the child is not trying to bully you; the tot has a want, a wish, a longing that is not conscious. Don't thwart her young life.

Love her, and go on loving her.

SPANKING

I sometimes spank my girl of three when she is naughty. Is it right or wrong to spank?

It is not a question of right or wrong; in a way it is a case of cowardliness, for you are hitting someone not your own size. I don't suppose you hit your husband when he is being a nuisance. Is it because you wouldn't dare? He might strike you back. Of course, you're perfectly safe hitting

99

your child of three. She can't strike you back.

Spanking is an outlet for adult rage and frustration and hate. It would be interesting to discover if most spanking mothers are those who have an unsatisfactory sex life, or are frigid and therefore sex-hating. Happy mothers do not spank; they do not need to, for their state of well-being is unconsciously conveyed to the child. Tradition and public opinion postulate that children are automatically loved by their parents; but if a man and wife have ceased to love each other, the children may be reared in an unhappy and unloving atmosphere.

Many a child is naughty deliberately, but unconsciously. *"Mother does not love me, and if I can't get her love I'll get her hate, for I must get some important reaction from her."*

Instead of spanking the child, it would be far better if the parent sat down and pondered what she herself was doing that was wrong. *"Is my life only an existence? Did I sacrifice my career on the stage for the sake of these brats who make my life a hell?" "I am now getting on into my late thirties. My husband, I know, looks at younger women. . . . Leave that thing alone, child. Take that!"* No discontented mother can bring up her family well; she may inspire fear, but not love.

What happens when you spank your child? For one thing, you put fear into the child, a thing no one has a right to do. For another, you lose his love. The contrite affection he shows after a beating is false, insincere, inspired by rejection.

The worst mother is she who cries: "I don't love you any more." If there is such a thing as a mortal sin, that is it. Every child seeks love and security; every spanking is a deep psychological shock. The poor child knows nothing about projection; he doesn't realize that Father had a bad day at the office with his boss; he doesn't realize that Dad's anger is displaced anger—the anger he dared not show in the office. The child does not know that his mother may be sex starved, or that she may have developed a sex fixation on someone in her infancy—possibly her father—and is therefore incapable of having a good love life with her husband.

When the boy is spanked for coming in with mud on his clothes, he does not know that his mother is afraid of what the neighbors will think, for many a child is punished simply to satisfy neighborly opinion. You see it in railway carriages when the mite rushes along the corridor. *"I must show these people that my child has been well brought up,"* thinks the mother. . . . Spank!

I am not forgetting that children can be a nuisance to even the most balanced mother—their constant squabbling, their fingering of all the things the adult values. The squabbling usually is inspired by jealousy; and in most families, there is a lot of jealousy. Furthermore, the unconscious jealousy is increased by the mere fact that a parent cannot love, no matter what he says, every one of his children with equal fervor. A parent will prefer one child over another, and the child will feel this although he may not be conscious of it.

If there is a remedy for spanking, it lies in self-examination on the part of the irritated adult. Spanking is symbolic castration. It breaks the will, it induces hate, it can ruin a life. Millions who were spanked in childhood go on spanking their own children later on. Perhaps we punish because we are a Christian civilization. If you sin, punishment awaits you in the here and now, and Hell awaits you in the future.

Parents who spank are little people, hating people, cowardly people. I wish parents could acquire some consciousness of what they really are . . . poor, undeveloped, unhappy people clothed in a tawdry authority which they are too ungrownup to use decently. Most parants, alas, cannot help being as they are, for they are the victims and products of a home and school education that was ignorant of child nature.

DESTRUCTIVENESS

We live in a small three-room apartment, the best we can afford. We have a few knick-knacks and mementos which we treasure, and we are in a constant dither lest Junior climb up on a chair, reach up, and break these very nice things. We know that, ideally, we should have a separate room for the little boy where he could not destroy anything of value to us. As parents dedicated to Summerhill ideas, we are deeply concerned about saddling him with restrictions about not to touch this or that. Have you any advice?

Here we have a universal problem, that of the gulf between juvenile and adult values. In every home, parents have to tell a child to leave something alone—the cat with its tempting tail, the cooking gadgets, the electric plugs. In the case at hand, the best solution would be for the parents to park all the valued things in closed cupboards or on high shelves.

In a way, your child has more realistic values than you have. To a parent. ornaments, photographs, etc. have a

static value; the disappearance of these mementos and arti-
facts would, in most cases, not actually make a scrap of
difference in the real day-to-day happiness of the average
adult. To the child, the adored objects are things to move,
to do something with—the delight in hearing a glass pitcher
smash on the floor, for example.

Generally, it is the mother who overvalues things; it is
she who buys vases that mean little to the father, and less
than nothing to the child. Nearly every house is cluttered up
with bric-a-brac that very often is not even ornamental . . .
the family photograph on the mantelpiece, the bowl that
Aunt Mary sent last Christmas. I almost feel like saying
that it would be a good thing to give Junior the whole lot
to prance on, though, I admit, this is beside the point.

The real point is that millions of children are constantly
sacrificed to things and to stupid taboos: *Sit up straight at
table. Don't start to eat until all are served. Don't dare spill
anything on the kitchen floor.*

It is all a matter of values. A parent might well ask
himself: *Which would I miss most—Junior—or that crystal
decanter?* Put the decanter away until the child is grown,
and you will have both your child and your precious piece.

Our boy of six likes to break windows. We might encourage him to go on doing so but we cannot afford to pay for them. What can we do?

At the moment, Summerhill has such a boy of six. He
has had a rather strict upbringing. I asked him if he broke
windows at home. "Yes, but I don't now because I got
whipped for it."

Obviously, this little fellow is seeking love; he is one of those typical cases where the unconscious thought is: *If I can't get love, I'll get hate.* Our staff do their best to show that little lad love; the window damage is followed by hugging and approval. Even our pupils do their best for him; in their tribunals, they never charge him with wanton destruction. They know what's going on underneath, and they sympathize with the poor tyke.

I have no idea of your home set-up, and can only guess that Junior deems himself neglected in some way. He is undoubtedly trying to win attention. I am certain that punishment will only make him behave worse.

Even if you could afford it, I would be against your joining him in breaking glass. I once knew a schoolmaster who had an outbreak of glass smashing in his school. He joined in the fun; and the whole class burst into tears for they knew he was doing something he didn't believe in. When Homer Lane, the great educator, joined his delinquent lads in destruction, he was a smiling schoolboy himself. Lane empathized with the underprivileged, deprived boy. He had the power to put himself in the place of the destroyer. Lane acted via emotion. When dealing with children, one should not act because one thinks the method is right: one must *feel* the method is right.

My practical advice to you is: give the boy a drum and a whistle and as many metal toys as it will take for him to make one hell of a row. That might serve as a full outlet. And then, parents, you can set about worrying about what to do to placate the neighbors. But most important of all: give the kid as much love as you are capable of.

Too few parents ask the proper questions: *Why is my boy breaking windows? Why is he stealing? Why does my boy find joy in destroying?* If one accepts the psychology of William Golding's *Lord of the Flies,* the answer is easy. A boy is a young devil; he has to be made good by adult example and by punishment and through character-molding.

My answer is that a young devil—when free to be himself without outside compulsion—becomes a social human being. Given time, of course.

If a boy is hateful and destructive, he is protesting against something in the home: lack of parental love, or too many stupid and unnecessary restrictions. *Don't put your elbows on the table, boy.*

Let me emphasize: NO HAPPY CHILD DESTROYS. Wherever there is a destructive child, the parents should ask themselves: *Why isn't my child happy?*

BULLYING AND FIGHTING

I am a working mother. My five-year-old attends a nursery school when I'm at work. His teacher says that he is very rough with the other children, hitting them and grabbing their things away. How can I make him stop doing this?

You can not. All you can do is to sit down and ask yourself what has happened to him to make him aggressive.

Have you spanked him, raged at him? Are you happily married? Is his aggression an imitation of yours or of your husband's? He must have a vague notion that you do not love him enough or you wouldn't park him in a school all day. But that is a reality that nothing can be done about.

How can I answer a question like this when I do not know whether he has brothers or sisters who bully him at home? I have no idea what sort of a school the boy is at; most likely one in which the adults make all the rules. But the school is never as important as the home; a child's behavior is conditioned by the home.

Self-regulated children seem to have less aggression than other children. By and large, I do not see them bullying, or destroying, or fighting. Aggression means pushing yourself forward without caring for others; that is what a young child will do. *Me, too! Me first!* But time cures that kind of aggression—if the child feels free.

Homer Lane used to put it this way: A small child wants to eat the *entire* apple; if told to share that apple with his sister, he naturally hates his sister. Later in life, it may give that same boy more pleasure to share the apple with his sister than to eat it all himself.

During the gangster age—8 to 14—boys often bully and destroy. At Summerhill, one boy of nine when asked why he always hit a girl of six, answered: "Because she looks like my bloody sister." In girls, on the other hand, the aggression takes the form of bitchiness.

When teachers are aggressive, their pupils follow suit. When parents punish, they are making their children aggressive. The most aggressive pupils I ever have had are those who have been most disciplined at home and school. When insulted or denigrated, a bright lad can strike back with a repartee, but a dull boy can only hit back with his fist. Army-sergeant bullies are usually stupid men—grown up children.

In freedom, a child's aggression comes out, and is expended in time. Under discipline, where does the aggression go to? The hate stays buried deep down in the personality, ready to come out later in anti-life attitudes, sex repression of others, and quarrelsomeness. The only way of diminishing aggression in our world is to grant freedom to the child to develop in his own way and in his own time.

Your child's companions will slowly but surely put him in his place if they are his equal in age. Ask the teacher for time and plead for patience.

You, his mother, must try to show the tyke that he is loved and not hated. One cannot get far by talking to a child of five; he will not understand reason—only action. But if the action is anger, or slapping, or scolding, he will vent the hate you've shown him on someone at school he can hit and get back at.

My three-year-old is very passive when other children hit him or take his toys away. He doesn't defend himself; he just cries. I don't like to intervene, nor do I like to teach him to hit back. Yet it hurts me to see him constantly bullied and hurt. How can I help him?

Only by keeping him away from bullying children. You cannot teach a child of three to fight back; nor, if you could, would it be good for him.

For whatever reason, some children are tough and insensitive; others are not at all aggressive. But, Mother, better for your son to be a young Gandhi than a young Hitler.

I know it is hard and painful to see your child suffer. It's strictly up to you to give him as much protection from the bullies as you can.

If he were ten instead of three, I'd suggest a few boxing lessons.

When playing together, the kids on my block often strike each other. My youngster is getting socked around—and plenty. Some parents in my neighborhood have counselled their children to hit back. I am not very happy about this approach but I don't know what to tell my son. What do you suggest?

When children—or for that matter adults—turn the other cheek, that cheek is usually hit hard. A Jesus can be a true pacifist, but most people cannot be pacifists—the brutes win. Six million non-resisting Jews died in the gaschambers; peaceful Tibet was ravished by the Chinese; infants die a terrible death when planes drop napalm. The world hits, and keeps on hitting.

We have to face the bitter truth. Boys who have been disciplined with fear discharge their hate by hitting other boys smaller than themselves.

The fact is that the old are better protected than the young; almost every peaceful householder would use an iron poker on a dangerously armed intruder; we can even ring for the police. But little Willie, bullied by a gang of young toughs, has no protection.

Yes, teach him to box; or teach him jiu-jitsu or whatever, but teach him how to protect himself in a world peopled by aggressors.

LYING

My son of ten is a great liar. How can I cure him? I have tried spanking him, sending him to bed, depriving him of a meal, all to no purpose.

Why try to cure him? Aren't you a liar yourself, good lady? Did you lie to the boy about where babies come from? Did he ever see you look out of the window and exclaim: "Here comes that awful Mrs. Smith," and later, meet Mrs. Smith and see you give her a big smile with a "Glad to see you, Mrs. Smith." What I am really asking is whether his lying is an aping of his mother.

But assuming that you are a very good mother, I suggest that your son may have a gifted imagination that one day may make him a successful novelist. I am ruling out a common cause of lying, a fear of being found out.

The boy may feel inferior—is he under-sized? He may be compensating for his insignificance by making himself important. *"I saw 10 funerals today."* He saw only one.

Whatever the cause of his lying, your punishment is a very dangerous thing. You are adding fear to his complex. Furthermore, you are killing his natural love for his mother. You are giving him a feeling of guilt.

You are making him say nay to life. For all you know, he may be lying to hide his guilt about masturbation. You may have tried to fashion him into a good little boy, and this is his protest.

You cannot cure him. I have often "cured" a pathological liar by demanding that he must answer with a lie every question I asked him. I think now that I did wrongly. I may have nipped his creativity in the bud.

Telling a lie is a minor peccadillo: living a lie is a major tragedy.

What do you do with a child who exaggerates the facts? My son is not an outright liar, but he certainly stretches the

truth. He will say he scored 18 points in a basketball game when he scored only 8. He'll say he got B-plus in biology when he really got B.

I'd do nothing. The boy apparently feels so inferior that he must enhance his ego by being the big shot. He is only doing what we all do in one way or another.

The whole story is set forth in Sinclair Lewis's *The Man Who Knew Coolidge,* a lovely tale of a salesman who was in Coolidge's class at college. He was always boasting of his friend the President. It transpired once—and only once—that Coolidge had spoken to him on the campus, making a remark about the weather. And that is the story of us all.

Your boy is not at all abnormal. His aim is to make himself important. You should try to think out why life for the boy is so drab and why he feels so stunted that he must stretch the facts to endow himself with importance.

Then again, that boy may be a coming novelist or a playwright. Never curb a child's imagination: his school education does that job most efficiently.

You might well just sit down quietly and try to remember the many occasions on which you exaggerated the truth. For all I know, the lad may be imitating his parents.

"Uncle Fred?" says Mother, "Oh, he is in a good government job." Fred is in Sing Sing.

Parents, examine yourselves, and laugh at yourselves, and leave the young boaster alone.

My husband and I are distraught. We haven't any idea why our boy of 12 is such a boaster, a liar, and—I say it with

shame—a bully. Our home atmosphere, which is at least normally congenial, should not have produced these characteristics in the boy. Have you any advice?

Dear parents, why worry so much? We are all liars, even though we are often unconscious of our lying.

A friend of mine is learning to play the violin; he has no musical talent at all. Recently, he asked: "How do you think I'm getting on?"

"Fine," I lied glibly.

Good manners make most of us lie. Most children lie because they are afraid of the consequences if they tell the truth.

And who isn't a boaster? It is mostly politeness that makes us repress our desire to show off. Who is so unegoistic as to feel no thrill when he sees his face on a TV screen? But, of course, excessive boasting always betrays a great feeling of inferiority. If your boy for whatever reason feels inferior, you won't be helping things by showing him up. Forbidding him to boast won't cure his inferiority.

I once had a boy of 13 who boasted all day long; his hearers were so bored by his talk that they left him outside their group. When he realized what the score was, he modified his boasting. That was coming to grips with the best teacher—reality. Had that lad been lectured by parents and teachers, he would have simply kept his desire to boast parked until he found a suitable occasion to boast before his own age group. Lecturing never cured anything.

Bullying is a more serious affair. The child of today lives in an atmosphere of violence. Our comics, our radio, our movies reek with sadism. The child who reacts to these hate media must be he who has hate problems of his own.

Do his brothers and sisters lord it over him? Has he been brought up in a religion of fear? Do his parents hate each other? Has he been punished for masturbation? Does he hate his school? If the parents can afford it, a few talks with a good therapist might help a lot.

STEALING

My son of nine is stealing from shops. What can I do?

There is really no simple answer; each case is different. I am convinced that most stealing by children is due to a lack of love at home. If you have not given your son love for nine years, it is hard to say just how to make up for the deficiency over night.

Every child steals at one time or another. Most adults will smuggle if they can—a customs official once told me he kept his eye on parsons. A good parent will not make a fuss when Tommy steals a quarter from Mommy's purse.

It is the moral parent who is so dangerous. *"You wicked boy. Didn't you know you were doing wrong?"* I wonder how many delinquents have had moral mothers. It is highly dangerous to give a child a feeling of guilt. The better way is to say: "Tommy, you took a dollar from me; give it back to me, it's mine." This is valid. What is entirely invalid is to take the moral attitude that he is a bad, sinful boy.

No one is completely honest. We adults are such humbugs about honesty. How many of us are honest because of fear of the police? If we make a long distance call from a telephone booth, and the operator says "Your three minutes are up, sir. I'll let you know what the extra charges are when you have completed your call," how many of us won't just hang up when through talking and stalk out of the phone booth? Oh, it's only the telephone company, and one is certainly allowed to cheat that colossus. Honesty, be hanged!

Many a father who cheats the Income Tax Bureau will wallop his son for stealing.

On a recent train trip, the regular seats were all taken, so I went into a Pullman, ready to pay the difference. In a journey of several hours no one came around to examine my ticket. Did I go to the ticket office and say: "I travelled in a parlor car; I want to pay the difference." It is so easy to rationalize, so easy for me to argue, "If the railway company wants to lose money by not having its men collect fares, why should I help them out?" Yes, we're all so piously honest until the chips are down.

Freedom breeds a tremendous amount of tolerance; at least three parents have complained to me that Summerhill made their children *too* tolerant. In 45 years, I have never seen a child jury at Summerhill punish a young thief for stealing; all they demand is that the thief pay back what he stole. Adult juries please copy.

Alfred is just a little past 12. Last week, I got a note from the principal of his school that the boy was caught stealing some fruits from a grocery store. He was labeled as a thief. His punishment was to stay in after school an extra hour each day for 30 days. I know he'll live through this extremely severe punishment, but I don't want the boy to feel guilty for the rest of his days and writhe under the shame of being a thief. What can I do to help the situation?

I would have given the boy a dollar reward for his enterprise—but then, I am concerned with the boy and not with the stolen fruit.

The principal's job should have been to try to find out *why* your boy stole. That worthy apparently is ignorant of the truth that hate never cured anything. His punishment was plain hate.

Most children steal at one stage or another; most are lucky enough not to be caught. Severe punishment can make a boy an enemy of society. *"They punished me badly, and to hell with them; I'll fight them forever, and be anti-social forever."* Fortunately, most boys are healthy and do not develop this extreme reaction.

Teachers, as a rule, are ignorant men. They know little of psychology. They take the easy way. For them, punishment, at least, shelves the responsibility of investigating the *cause*. Punishment gives the teacher a quiet life. The damnable thing is that such treatment is universal in schools in all lands.

But, my dear lady, do ask yourself if you are giving the boy enough love. I am convinced that most young thieves steal love symbolically.

In Summerhill, of course, we get occasional stealing but we deal with it without introducing punishment. All the school community asks is that the money be repaid. And I always warn every young thief that if he steals outside the school, the police may be called in and then I won't be able to protect him. For the law, like that principal, seeks punishment.

A bold parent would have asked that principal if *he* ever stole when he was 12? A bad teacher is always one who has forgotten his childhood, and therefore is completely out of touch with the young.

You ask what you can do to help? Love him, hug him, approve of him! Tell him frankly that his teacher is wrong.

SULKING

My boy, John, is a sulker. He is 11 years old. Any time either my husband or I ask him to do anything that doesn't suit his mood, he grumbles and sulks. As a matter of fact, he sulks whether the directive comes from us or from anyone else. Some of his friends call him "Cry Baby" because he stands off and sulks when he doesn't get his own way in a game. Have you any suggestions?

No, I have no suggestions.

But why worry? Most folks go into a sulk when they are irritated or unhappy. A sulking boy feels he has not been well treated. He cannot hit back against the offending adults; his sulking represents his repressed aggression against authority. If he sulks at home, his method of resentment will naturally carry over to his games with his companions.

Sulking is an interesting phenomenon. A wife criticizes her husband. Instead of hitting back, he sulks . . . *"I'll pay you back, you damned nagger, I won't speak to you."* Sulking takes the place of hitting back.

If I were you, I should ask myself what I am doing to him to rouse his ineffectual aggression. The boy has some grievance; he must feel that he is odd man out.

TELEVISION

Jimmy is a nice kid, lovable and kind, but he sits around all day glued to the TV set. He doesn't read a thing. What can I do?

Tut, tut, we cannot put the clock back. TV has come to stay.

TV has slain much reading. When I was a boy I read Scott's *Ivanhoe*, skipping the descriptions of scenery. Today, a boy can get the story in 75 minutes on TV.

If a boy spends his day sitting on a bench studying what does not interest him, he will tend to continue the process at home and sit passively in the fantasy world that so much of TV provides. The lad is escaping; it is easier to escape by watching a screen than by reading a book. But nothing can be done about it, for you cannot compel a boy to read or to use his hands making things.

No cause for alarm, my dear parent, the phase will not last forever. If the boy has any guts, energy, and ambition, he'll be off and doing—when he is ready.

I should like to see an experiment done in a school. Make the whole day one long TV show and then see if the pupils will turn to making things with wood or metal or clay or needles as an escape from passivity.

You say he does not read; I wonder how much that matters. I have known men who read everything; they were walking encyclopedias and always had an answer when facts were asked for. But they knew much and understood little. Ah! But I'm prejudiced; for I prefer doers to readers any day. I myself would rather buy a lathe than the Encyclopaedia Britannica.

Do not badger Jimmy by saying, "Why don't you get away from that TV set and read a book." This could change Jimmy from being "lovable and kind" into a rebellious boy.

FOOD AND EATING

My son is 11 years old and is more than 50 pounds over-
weight. Should I force him to go on a diet?

You can take a horse to the water but you can't make
him drink. I very much doubt if anything can be done with
the boy at home. No boy can feel happy eating a diet salad
when he sees the rest of the family tucking away the bacon
and eggs.

If a child does not see the necessity of something, it is
very difficult to get him to change his ways. If your boy were
adolescent and the girls laughed at his fatness, he would
have a motive to slim; but a boy of 11 has no motive to get
thin. But why so much worry? I have seen children who
were fat at 10 and slim at 20.

Although malfunctioning of glands is extremely rare,
his obesity may have little to do with his diet. Only a medical man can judge whether or not his glands are properly
functioning. But if a doctor tells you the boy's body is functioning normally, then leave him alone.

My boy of six is extremely picky about food. It seems the
only things he likes to eat are hamburgers, steak, and ice
cream. We can't afford steak often, and my husband and
I are just about sick and tired of eating hamburgers. What's
the solution?

If your boy is fussy about food, try to give him what
he likes to eat, but don't cater to him at the expense of forcing every member of the family to adapt their tastes to his.

Your boy wants to live on hamburgers? Well and good! But that shouldn't mean that everyone else in the family must live on hamburgers. It is wrong to force a child to eat what he does not want to eat; it is equally wrong to force a family to eat what only one member of that family prefers.

At Summerhill, we have a boy who refuses to eat mutton, or roast beef, or sausages, or vegetables. All he wants is a plateful of potatoes and butter. We give him his spuds every day—because they're easy to prepare. But if he demanded chow mein or duck a l'orange, we wouldn't dream of complying. To judge from past experience, the day will soon come when that boy will want to eat what the other children are eating. But however that might be, it would be ludicrous if we were to say, "Jimmy likes only potatoes and butter, so all you other kids will now live on his diet." To me it sounds equally ludicrous for you to say, "My son likes only hamburgers, so from now on my husband and I are going to feed on hamburgers, day in and day out."

My practical advice is give the boy his own way within reason which certainly means that his diet must fall within your financial capabilities. Furthermore, unless your son is to be spoiled and made king of the roost, he should be made to adapt to the needs of the other people in your family. The matter should be handled on a compromise basis: Monday, hamburgers; Tuesday, fish; Wednesday, macaroni and cheese—something like that. If Junior won't eat the non-hamburger meals, then he simply must do without. Don't worry, he won't starve. He'll feed on bread and water; he'll rummage in the ice-box or in the pantry; he'll find something or other to allay his hunger, but he won't starve.

I have a feeling that a food complex in a child has some

element of protest within it. He may be using his special likes and dislikes to proclaim, *"I am the big shot in this joint. What I say goes. Pass the ice cream."* Johnny's food fad should set you to try to discover just what is the boy's hidden motivation. What do his particular dislikes symbolize?

THUMB-SUCKING

My dentist tells me that I must do something about my boy's thumb-sucking. The boy is 12. How can I get him to stop it?

Thousands of children have sucked their thumbs and have gone on living normal lives. I don't know how to stop the habit. All methods of prohibition seem to me wrong: tying up the hand, putting nasty-tasting stuff on the thumb, spanking, lecturing. They all lead nowhere, or rather they may lead to somewhere unpleasant.

Thumb-sucking must have some connection with infant sucking. Like biting the nails, it is a harmless symptom of some earlier phase that was never lived out. Suppress it and you may drive the boy back to worse habits—messing his pants, for instance.

I cannot see that thumb-sucking is important enough to fuss over. Every child gets over the habit in time.

SLEEP

Sam is a restless sort of kid. He just won't go to bed on time. Most kids of ten are asleep by 10 o'clock, but Sam doesn't fall asleep. He shitts around in bed for at least an hour or two every night. And he complains to us, "Why do you put

me to bed when I can't sleep?" Should we permit him to roam the house until 11 or so, or until he feels really sleepy?

I should be inclined to allow him to go to bed when he wants to. Nature itself will afford him regulation in time—possibly in a short time at that.

My child refuses to go to sleep. If I let him stay up as long as he likes, the next day he is droopy and very tired at school. If I insist that he go to his room when it is time for bed, he goes but does not sleep, and again is tired all through the school day. How can I train him to go to sleep at a decent hour?

No child wants to go to bed and leave the grown-ups sitting watching TV. This boy may have some fear of being alone; or he may simply want to annoy his parents, if they are strict with him; or bed may mean to him masturbation and guilt, something to postpone.

The lad may be of the introverted type that never plays games or runs about. The tiredness at school may have some other cause—perhaps hate of lessons. There could be a thousand reasons for his not wanting to go to bed. Sending him to his room seems to have no effect, and should be abandoned.

In Summerhill, we sometimes get such a child. The community now and then votes that he be exempt from the bedtime rules and that he can sit up all night. The young night-owl does so for at most two nights, and then he accepts the general bedtime rule. I have never heard of this method being used in a home but it might be worth trying, for compulsion is hopeless. You can test this theory by watching carefully at weekends to see if the lad is tired when there is no schooling. You may also want to consult a good psychologist.

TOYS

My little son gets too many presents from friends. He received as many as 20 at Christmas, played with a few for a short time, and now they clutter up the room. Should I refuse to let people give him toys?

Toys are 90 per cent a waste of money and material. Especially, the mechanical ones. According to Vance Packard, the U.S.A. is one vast waste machine with gadget superseding gadget as the commercial agents decree.

I see children getting so many things without ever having to lift a hand to get them. The result is that these gadgets are often of no value to the child. So many expensive presents are seldom appreciated for long. How many guitars, pleaded for by Beatle fans, lie unused in homes?

I fear that when greatly expanded leisure comes to our society, so very, very few will be capable of using that leisure. Today, for the masses, leisure means dog tracks, Bingo, football watching, TV watching, none of these pursuits being in the least creative.

But as for your little boy, I don't see how you are to prevent his getting gifts. Forbid them, and he will have a grouse against you. Besides, he'll feel inferior to his friends who receive gifts. After all, the toys will do him no harm, and the kindly friends will go on being satisfied with their Christmas giving.

Nay, don't forbid the gifts. Collect the junk, and later on send it all to an orphanage.

A year ago, Stevie plagued me for a punching bag. I bought it for him. After three weeks he seemed to tire of it and then badgered me for a small bowling set. I got this for him too, but his interest in it was short-lived. Now he says he is in earnest—he wants me to buy him a bicycle. Since he is somewhat puny and needs a build up of his physical self-confidence, I am eager to have him indulge in athletics. But I see that in the past he has not used what he has asked for. He is making a terrible fuss over my refusal to buy him a bike. Are there any conditions I should impose before making the purchase, or any promises to extract, or what?

No conditions, no promises! Your previous gifts weren't fundamentally important enough for him; they kept him stationary in a room. A bike will let him explore the world around him. It promises adventure; the other gadgets did not.

But be prepared: he probably will ride the bike constantly for a week and then may forget to take it indoors and leave it out in the rain. They all do, bless 'em.

But don't worry about that. It is only metal that costs some money, and money can be replaced.

Parents should never lay down conditions. *"If you pass this exam well, I'll give you a bike."* Bad, very bad. And stupid, too. I can see the twinkle in the eyes of my good friend Henry Miller if someone offered him a Rolls Royce if he would sit down and write a book. Henry would laugh and throw down his pen.

See that the boy gets good instruction about road safety. Handle the matter pleasantly; and if it all doesn't work out according to your blueprint, no recriminations. The boy is far more important than the bike.

FANTASY

Should I tell my child about Santa Claus?

Dear old Santa! I thought the decrepit oldster was dead, and that Christmas cards were but memorials to his memory. These days, I never meet a child who believes in him; but then, I seldom meet unimaginative parents. In these days of steam heat and gas heaters, it must be difficult to explain that Santa comes down the chimney. In a world populated by jets, a child with some imagination will wonder how the red-nosed reindeer manage to avoid collisions and fly unscathed.

By all means tell your child stories, but tell them as stories—not as facts. I have the impression that any parent who would hoodwink his child about Santa would deceive his child about birth and tell him the baby was brought by a stork. Such a parent is likely to tell his child that he will go to hell if he masturbates, or lose his tongue if he tells lies.

Better bury old Santa, and let him rest in peace; there is enough fiction abroad in the world as things are. If you feel compelled to dress up as Santa, your child should know who is behind the white beard and the red cloak. Your child should also see his mother filling the stockings—no bunk about miracles.

My daughter, Carol, now nine, seems to sit and daydream all day long. Is fantasy bad for a child?

What is fantasy anyway? It is wishful thinking. All of us fantasy, no matter what one's age. I have just recently dropped my fantasy that someone with a name like Rockefeller would read my books and endow Summerhill with a million dollars, but that fantasy did not make me ignore the reality of my work. The man who built the Empire State Building must have made a daydream picture of it before he started to build. I daydreamed about writing this book.

Heaven is a fantasy that comforts many people, especially the bereaved. Humanists have a fantasy of an earthly paradise that is not likely to exist in our time. Granted that most fantasies do not result in fulfillment. So if all we grown-ups fantasy, why shouldn't a child fantasy, too? Fantasy is natural and normal. Abolish fantasy, and all stories would be too dull to read.

In any case, even if you think that fantasy is bad for a child, you cannot do anything about it.

Problems of Adolescence

STAYING OUT LATE

I am scared. My daughter is 17 and she has got into the company of young people who drive fast cars and go drinking and petting and maybe more than petting. She comes in late, sometimes early in the morning. She takes no notice of what my husband and I say. What can we do?

I fancy that hundreds of thousands of parents could ask this question. Parents must face the hard truth that they cannot do a thing about their adolescent children. Prohibitions and lectures make the situation worse. They arouse all the hidden resentment so many adolescents have for their parents.

The bitter truth is that home is too dull for the young. There used to be an illustrated advertisement for a miniature billiard table. "Keep your boys at home in the evening." I doubt if that table kept one boy at home. Home to parents is a quiet place with comfy chairs, a TV set, a library, a place to relax from the house chores, a refuge from the office. Youth does not want to relax; it wants movement. Hence the pop craze. Youth wants young company, dance, music, a few drinks; youth seeks first and foremost the company of its peers. The wise parent will accept all this—will not only tolerate it, but try to approve of it.

I guess that your question really means: *I am scared that my daughter will get pregnant.* The best way to pregnancy is making sex the forbidden fruit. Girls reared with a sense of freedom seldom get pregnant.

I once believed that the strict authority exercised by parents over their children was primarily due to jealousy of the life and the verve and the beauty of youth. I am not so sure now. Parents are genuinely afraid. The world today is full of alarms and excursions. Our civilization is very, very sick, and the forces (Vietnam, Rhodesia, race hatred) that may soon bring the third and last war have their counterpart in our social society: an alarming increase in crime, the increased taking of dope, the rat race for money and status. We live in an unbalanced world, certainly a most dangerous world. And the older generation has been left behind. Most parents cannot understand why a million hysterical girls scream at the Beatles, or why youth rejects the old cultures and the old religions. Huxley's *Brave New World* is a fearsome world that lives for the moment. I said to a lad of 15: "What will you be when you grow up?" He grinned. "You mean *if* I grow up."

The parental alarm is a rational one, but is it necessary? Parents who have developed a home atmosphere of mutual trust need not worry if their girl comes home late. If our own daughter at 16 had come home at two in the morning, my wife and I would not have thought of asking her where she had been. First of all, she would have told us without our asking.

The question really boils down to: Are you scared about your daughter because of your own lack of balance and faith? Are you projecting your own fear of life on to your daughter?

I grant the objective factors, the dangers of her being driven around in a car by drunken youths, of her getting mixed up with a dope crowd, of being seduced when under the influence of alcohol. But I contend that a girl, brought up freely and with love, will not go off the deep end just because she happens to be outside of her home.

The best way to make her go wrong is to lecture her and nag her and bully her. Just give her the idea that sex is a forbidden topic; and if you are religious, be sure to impress her that sex is a sin against God. Then you can practically count on her rebellion. And thought, under such stimulus, may give way to action.

Our daughter Susan is 17. The other night she came home at five o'clock in the morning, and she found me and my husband sitting there biting our fingernails, worrying whether to call the police station, absolutely in a sweat worrying as to what had happened to her. Well, here we were in this furor, and in she marches. After we reproached her with her staying out late and not calling, she belittled our anxiety and indignantly shouted, ''Well, what's the matter, don't you trust me?'' Frankly, we didn't know what to answer to this outburst. Is there anything to say? Perhaps underneath it all we are worried about the girl going wrong in some way, though there must be a real honest-to-goodness anxiety, too, about her safety when she stays out until 5 A.M.

Oh, dear me! So many questions from America that seem to ask the same thing—*"I have lost my child, and what can I do about it?"*

If my daughter stayed out all night, neither my wife nor I would ask her where she had been. She trusts us, and we trust her. It's as simple as that! We are not the least bit worried that she will get drunk or pregnant.

Mind you, I don't know the environment of this particular girl; I can imagine an environment in which any parent would be worried. Going out with callow youths who drive the old man's car under a load of liquor, going out with a crowd of dope-takers or alcoholic addicts—yes, it can be very frightening. I discount the sex angle somewhat, for seduction always involves the agreement of two. If a girl has had a good grounding on sex, her chances of seduction are small unless she is under the influence of drink. But so many homes are so bad that the young seek all their pleasures outside the home. The 5 A.M. return may have been a protest against always having been treated as an irresponsible baby. If parents will not understand their child's interests, they are asking for trouble.

The compulsive family is the greatest danger to youth. The steel bands that parents forge to bind their children to their own old-fogey notion of life are steel traps in which the parents eventually get caught. Such parents kill the love and joy in the child from cradle days. Such parents inhibit natural expression and natural desire.

But how can we blame such parents when their entire education never touched the most important job in the world—the job of bringing up children. The other day I heard a girl of 26 cry: "I took my B.A. degree with honors in math—but I wish to heaven someone had taught me how to deal with this baby of mine."

A parent is a specialist who never had any training as a specialist. He shoves the whole load of his own ideas of religion and of politics and of morals on to his offspring and he is then surprised and embittered when he discovers that his children resent the burden and that he has lost all contact with his family.

Delinquency commences in the nursery. Rear a child in an anti-life way, scold the child, spank the child for messing his pants—and you're on the road to creating a neurotic. Teach your child to be "good," teach your child to fear you and to fear God, pervert all the child's natural instincts, and if you get a problem child, you should know why.

The usual answer I get is: "But haven't all kids been molded, been moralized too; then why do only a few become delinquents?" A sensible question. I cannot answer it. Who can? Of course, there's always the economic factor. Perhaps the impact of a poor environment on a child of a certain fragility produces the miserable result. A boy is born on a mean street. His home has no culture, no books, no serious conversation. His parents are ignorant; they slap him around and yell at him. He attends a school where strict discipline and dull subjects drive him to distraction. His playground is the street corner. His companions are boys who, due to the same or similar causes, are also unhappy. His ideas about sex are pornographic.

He sees other people with money and cars and all sorts of luxuries. He feels himself underprivileged, disadvantaged. At adolescence, he gets into a gang whose aim is to get rich quick at all costs.

How can we cure a boy with that kind of background? Our reform schools only dish out more of the discipline against which the boy has rebelled. The prison environment only increases his hate of life and of humanity.

Homer Lane proved that freedom can cure a delinquent, but there are few Homer Lanes around, and juvenile crime increases every year.

If every child were reared in the Summerhill way—in freedom—juvenile crime would decrease enormously. Freedom has to begin in the home—in fact, in *infancy*. But the vast majority of parents haven't the knowledge, the patience, nor the belief in the goodness of human nature to make their home a free home for the children they bring into this stark world.

As usual, I have wandered from the point. It is one of my major charms they tell me. A dull writer is a guy who sticks to the point, too often a blunt one.

Coming back to your daughter Susan. Parents, trust that girl of 17. Let her grow at her own pace and in her own time. Everytime you distrust her, you are losing another chunk of her natural love.

And by the way, lady, did you ever come home late when you were 17?

CURSING

My youngster has picked up some foul language on the street. He has never heard such words at home. While we understand that there is nothing vicious in words themselves, we are definitely embarrassed when he comes out with a phrase that makes all heads turn. In our society, such language is never used in public. We have told him that we personally don't care about his language, but that swearing in such an unbridled way abashes us before the neighbors. Somehow he just hasn't taken us too seriously. Even though he tries to curb his language, now and then some pretty awful things slip out. What should we do?

Unfortunately, you cannot break the rules of conventional society by telling your neighbors that they are a lot of prudish, hypocritical humbugs who probably privately

leer at sex pictures, snicker and rub their hands gleefully
when listening to dirty jokes—jokes that aren't funny—only
dirty—and use swear words in their bars and clubs.

I notice that when a chamber pot appears in a film
Summerhill children never laugh, whereas the whole movie
audience goes into fits of laughter. Very few sex stories are
funny; most are only filthy. I have heard hundreds in my
time and I have told hundreds, but today I can think of
only one dirty story that is funny. I can't put it in print—a
pity—for it is really not pornographic—it's funny! And
readers, please don't write and ask me what it is either.

I suggest that your boy should be advised to discrim-
inate between those who are pro-life and those who are
anti-life. The boy should be made conscious of the fact
that some people are shockable. A wise parent could go on
to explain that people are only shocked when they have an
obscene, perverted interest in sex.

My pupils use quite a lurid vocabulary. But if any boy
or girl uses a four-letter word at a Summerhill general meeting when visitors are present, he is reproved by the others.

I once had a new pupil of five. When she was packing
to go home for summer vacation, I happened to get in her
way. "Get out of my way, you bugger," she said.

"Susan," I said, "your mother likes Summerhill, but
your father doesn't. If you go home and call him a bugger,
he may take you away from here and send you to another
school."

At the end of the holidays, her older sister said: "Funny
thing happened at home. Susan didn't swear once."

Yet slowly, humbug is giving way. Twenty years ago,
one could not use the word *fuck* in writing. Even in Partridge's *Dictionary of Slang* it was *f—k*. When I was a boy

damn was *d—n;* and when Shaw made Eliza Doolittle say the word *bloody,* the English press printed it as *b—y.* The publication of *"Lady Chatterley's Lover"* and *"The Tropic of Cancer"* were milestones on the road to honesty.

The difficulty about juvenile swearing is that it so often is an imitation of adult swearing. Children hear men on the street use four-letter words freely and without context. If sex lost its morality and repression, four-letter words would have little point. Swear words are vulgar words because they belong to the language of the common people. A professor says *anus,* but a navvy says *arse.* Maybe we should teach our kids to swear politely and shout out *Fornication! Excrement! Micturation!*

Owing to my husband's employment, we have to live in an area, that to say the least, is not genteel. My little son has to seek his playmates among what, without snobbery, I call the working class. He comes home with rude words. What can I do to protect him?

I like that word *rude;* it has such a lovely Victorian sound. When I was at school, we read Gray's *Elegy in the Churchyard* where "the rude forefathers of the hamlet sleep." I thought they were buried in the section reserved for those who had used bad language.

Some one might, after reading your question, ask: "Is this lady a snob?" Nevertheless, I think you have a point, for a good job so often depends on a good accent and you want your son to learn to speak properly and not acquire a sloppy enunciation. In England, a Cockney or a Lancashire accent can damn an applicant for certain jobs. Yet, I surmise that you are more concerned about your son's morals, especially his sexual morals than you are about your boy's accent, for I am sure you shudder at four-letter words.

I really do not think the situation is serious. As children of the village schoolmaster, we talked the dialect of the village with the sons and daughters of ploughmen; but the moment we crossed the home threshold, I automatically talked what was then the Queen's English. The odd thing was that we kids never mixed the two languages.

So take hope. The Anglo-Saxon swear words I learned outside did not corrupt me. They won't corrupt your son. Words, in themselves, mean little. It's behavior that counts. Dear mother, your attitude to your boy will have far far more influence on his future than all the words in the universe.

My boy swears and curses. Is this normal?

Swearing has little to do with having a poor English vocabulary. I say *bloody* instead of *sanguinary;* I say *hell* instead of *Hades;* my pupils say *shit* instead of *excrement.* Why the Anglo-Saxon words are indecent I do not know, but I suspect that the ban on them is a snobbish one. A university professor says *sexual intercourse*—a sailor calls the same thing *fucking.* But nowadays, many intellectuals are coming around, too, to prefer the simpler expressions.

Swearing, at times, is merely expressive and has little implication. A Scottish ploughman will describe a chattering man as a "heverin' hoor," but the educated Scot will call the same fellow a "blethering bugger."

Swearing must be entirely due to repression. The four-

letter sex words are a healthy protest against our obscene
attitude to all things sexual, just as our blasphemous words
are a protest against the perversions of Christianity.

Is swearing normal? Whether it is or is not, imitation
is normal. Your boy is only repeating with gusto what he
has heard others say—with gusto.

DRIVING A CAR

Johnny is 17. In our state, he is permitted to drive with a
beginner's license. The lawmakers say he is old enough to
drive a car during daylight hours and under certain restrictions.

My husband and I don't believe that our son has suffi-
cient stability at his age to drive a car. Johnny thinks we are
a bunch of fuddyduds, and has conceived a great feeling
of persecution. His resentment against not being allowed
to do what the other boys do seems always present, and
the resentment seems to grow with each week. The fact is
that we are in mortal terror lest the boy get into a car and
kill himself in a road accident. What can we do?

Your question does not reveal how much skill Johnny
has, or if he knows the laws of the road.

Most accidents are caused by youths. Statistics show
that the fewest accidents are caused by men over 60.

Here is a difficult situation. Thwarted, Johnny will be
likely to drive another boy's car without your knowing it.
I don't know the boy's psychology. So many accidents must
be unconsciously intended. The aggressive type acts as if
he owns the road and no one else matters. *"I'll pass the lot
of them. I'll do what I like, and to hell with other drivers."*

And there's the show-off—especially if girls are in the car. *"See how I dodged that Caddy by a hair's breadth."*

If he were my son, I'd take him out a few times and sit beside him as he drove. If he overtook dangerously, or passed cars on curves, or broke the speed limit, I'd tell him frankly that he wasn't a good enough driver to drive my car.

But just forbidding won't help; on the contrary, it may do harm. *"I'll show 'em how well I can drive; I'll pass every car on the road."* Don't permit the revenge motive to enter into it. *"If I wreck the damn car, it will serve 'em right for their stupid prohibitions."* Nevertheless, I should certainly tell him that any accident, no matter how trivial, would mean the end of his driving the family car.

SMOKING

Our daughter, Janet, came home the other day puffing a cigarette. She is 17. Judging from her expression, I knew that she thought she was being smart. What's more, she knew that her act of open rebellion would antagonize me. Now I really don't care from a moral point of view whether or not she smokes—but I am concerned from a health angle.

The point of my letter is that I don't know how to cope with her adolescent rebelliousness and her need to prove that she is going to be her own boss and do what she darn well likes.

Janet is a sensible girl, and I feel that she would listen to reason if only the doors could be opened. But her need to repudiate me as an authority figure at this point in her life seems to be overwhelming; and I am floored by the prospect of getting her to discuss this matter with me with candor and reasonableness. Are we mothers beaten? Is there any open sesame by which I can get my daughter to talk to me as if I were just another human being and not a forbidding parent?

Dear lady, I don't know what to say to you. Janet is doing what most young things do—she's trying to cut her apron strings. But why did you never cut these strings yourself, long before Janet was 17?

All this antagonism of youth against age is unnecessary. I am sure that all this so-called Oedipus reaction would disappear if parents behaved humanly with their children. Parents will make themselves into little tin gods to be feared, respected, obeyed; no wonder that youth turns bitter and rebels.

Obviously, lady, you are out of touch with Janet and have been so from her cradle days on. There is little rebellion where there is nothing to rebel against. In too many homes it's parents versus children instead of parents *on the side of* children. For heavens sake, stop preaching to her now. Cigarettes will do her far less harm than her earnest conviction that her mother is someone who is always lecturing her and forbidding something or other. Leave her be —even if you happen in this instance to be right.

Smoking? I fear you can't do anything about that. You can't fight the huge tobacco interests with their millions of dollars for propaganda. Unfortunately, it can be no comfort to you to realize that the unconscious fear of the H-bomb accounts for, not only cigarette smoking, and other means sought for release of tension, but also for much juvenile crime. Your girl's unconscious speaks up and says: *"We are all going to die young, so let's have as good a time as we can."*

No, in the fearsome and unsafe world of today, it is of no use to preach to youth about such small inconsequentialities as dangers to health. In a sick world, so many must be sick.

My son is a high school lad. He's 16. Many of the boys in his group smoke clandestinely. Neither I nor my husband feel that there is anything morally wrong in smoking. The fact is that both of us smoke. We are heavily addicted to smoking through years and years of habit.

However, we both are now convinced that smoking is a pernicious habit and may be deleterious to health. The federal government has just made it mandatory for cigarette manufacturers to place a statement on each package that ill health may attend constant smoking. Today, almost everyone realizes that cancer of the throat is much more widespread among smokers than it is among non-smokers. In other words, we want to guard our boy against the health hazard of smoking.

Of course, he has a perfect right to say, "You smoke, why shouldn't I?" In what way can we approach the boy to get him to understand that our concern about his smoking is genuine and honest, and that we are not at all troubled by old-fashioned morality in relation to smoking. The fact that he is 16 doesn't matter. We wouldn't want him to smoke even if he were 36.

I see your difficulty. I smoke a lot myself, a pipe generally, and I always feel a bit of a humbug when I warn youth against lung cancer.

In our school parliament here at Summerhill, a child proposed that anyone be allowed to smoke at any age. I proposed an amendment—that only pipes and cigars be allowed. It was carried by a small majority. For three days, cigars were in evidence, but then the pocket money was all spent, and cigars disappeared.

Nor would it make much of a difference if all my staff and I were non-smokers. I know a school in which smoking is a punishable offense; and of course, a few boys sneak off to the woods and have a surreptitious puff or two. It's the law that makes the crime.

Frankly, I do not know what to say or do about smoking. Forbid smoking and it goes underground with all the magnetic attraction of forbidden fruit. Warn about its dangers, and youth turns a deaf ear. The big battalions of commerce are on the side of tobacco. You, the worried parent, are fighting a battle against great odds.

Incidentally, I have a theory about lung cancer. When I was a boy lots of folks smoked cigarettes but we never heard of lung cancer. Today, tobacco crops are sprayed with insecticides. For the most part, cigar and pipe smokers do not inhale, and so do not get the effect of the insecticide. But cigarette smokers inhale poisonous pesticide. My theory is prompted by that disturbing, even alarming book *Silent Spring*. But my theory will not help you, mother, to convince your son. So you might as well fold up your campaign and let him be.

DRINKING

My son, 18, has taken to drink. Every day after school, he stops off at a bar with some of his boy friends, and takes a slug of whisky. At this point, he is not a confirmed alcoholic nor anywhere near that stage, but I see the trend and I'm worried stiff. Is there anything I can do now?

When a lad of 18 takes to whisky, there is something sadly lacking in his immediate environment. To drink compulsively always denotes an escape from reality.

Of course, I have no idea of what his private troubles are. I think the best course would be to have him take some therapy—if he would agree; but it would be hopeless to send him to therapy if he opposed the idea. You, his parents, cannot possibly know the precise reasons that drive him to the bottle, but a good analyst might be able to make conscious some of the hidden miseries that make him seek the alcoholic escape.

A man supported by a good sound philosophy of life can feel courageous about his personal situation despite his daily round of troubles; but a man who feels inferior may have to drink to feel a similar courage. If a man is timid by nature, a few drinks may make him feel brave. If his daily environment is dull and tawdry, a few whiskies may catapult him into a more rousing world, a world in which he is someone of importance. The strong man takes a drink in his stride; the weakling must drink on and on because, when sober, the real world is just too much for him.

In a case of young alcoholism, the focus of attention must be: What are the inner demands that drive your boy to drink? Does he feel himself inferior to his mates? Have you, his parents, demanded too much from him? You should ask yourselves: *"What is our boy trying to forget? and why? What have* we *done to make him seek comfort in a bar? Have* we *really helped to make his life as full and as happy as possible?"* I have known instances of young men taking to drink because their parents kept nagging them about getting on in life . . . *"You must stick to your books if you want to succeed in life."*

The answers won't help you too much now—for the most part, they'll be coming too late.

No, in a case like this, I suggest psychological treatment.

I am a high school student in New York City. I am 16 years old. A strong social atmosphere prevails in the school I go to. I have been invited to co-ed parties by all my girl friends. It is really my turn now to have a party. My mother is willing to provide such a party, but she adamantly refuses to serve beer. At every one of the parties that I have been to, it is customary to serve beer, and the boys and girls expect to have beer at their parties. I myself am not so fond of beer, but I would feel deeply embarrassed if I didn't provide beer for those who want it. I have told my mother that unless she is willing to serve beer, I would rather not have the party at all. So far, she has remained as steadfast as the Rock of Gibraltar. Can you explain this to me?

If my daughter wanted to have a beer party, I'd gladly supply the beer. It may be that behind your mother's refusal lies a fear that alcohol will loosen your teenage self-control and then there may be a pregnancy. Could be, of course, yet were I your mother I'd risk the beer to retain your affection.

DRUG ADDICTION

You have probably heard in England about the surge of drug-taking that has gripped American youth. My son is a student at Berkeley University in California. There are reports of widespread drug addiction on American campuses, and the rumors include Berkeley. Is there anything that I can say to my boy to keep him from embarking on a course of drug-taking? I know that preaching, as such, won't help because it is evident to me that at his age he pooh-poohs the values of his parents, and thinks we are old fogies. We know that his attitudes and our attitudes toward sex are miles apart. Just lecturing him in moral terms about drugs won't do any good at all. But we would like to ward off the destruction that does attend so many young people who fall into drug addiction. Could you give me some approach?

You are honest, and at least you realize the futility of parental advice. The sad fact is that no one ever learns from the experience of another—in small things, yes, say in learning to do simple equations, but in emotional things, no.

Generally among the young, there seems to be little thought of saving for a rainy day. That attitude may stem from the more or less unconscious thought that life is too precarious. The advent of the H-bomb has had a deep effect on all youth; much of the present rebellion of youth may come from the thought that life may be short.

I said to a 17-year-old girl: "You are smoking a hell of a lot. Aren't you afraid of lung cancer?"

Her reply: "Not a bit. I won't live long enough; no one will."

And so with drugs. No one who has a full, creative life will seek drugs as an escape. At its base, the drug question is not how to stop the trade, but how to make society happy enough to make the taking of dope needless. I would be shocked if any of my old pupils took drugs. I think they are too well balanced, too free from conflicts that drive people to escape routes.

The root of drug taking is unhappiness, misery ultimately due to the conflict between unconscious desires and moral principles. Abolish the guilt we call sin, and the drug merchants will go bankrupt.

You suggest a deep division at home: "Our sex attitudes are miles apart." But why? Cannot you get yourselves up-to-date? Can't you drop your puritanical attitude to sex? Or would you rather retain your orthodox repressive position and see your son ruined by drugs?

I am told that there's a car sticker now current in the U.S.A. which reads "MAKE LOVE NOT WAR." *Hear! Hear!*

If your boy takes to drugs, he is escaping from something; I guess it is his home and its morality. It may be that your home is a sanctuary for a narrow religion, a killjoy religion; it may be a home in which you, his parents, seek too much ambition for the members of your family.

I am·sure that the happier the home, the less inclination to gather snow—if that is what the U.S.A. still calls dope.

There is a great deal of marijuana smoking in American colleges today. It's considered the thing to take a whiff of pot, as they call it. The medical authorities say that marijuana is not habit forming; but they add that when a youngster has experienced marijuana, he then wants to experience an even greater thrill and goes on to stronger drugs which are addictive and destructive. My daughter, who is 19, attended one of those marijuana parties. Our relationship is pretty solid and she told me about it. But although the confidence between us is strong, I am nevertheless powerfully worried. She says that she just had to do it this once, but has no intention of ever doing it again. I suppose it is pointless for me to write you and ask you what can be done, but as I said before, I am ridden with anxiety.

I should guess that most young folks who experiment with marijuana once or twice do not become addicts, but I appreciate your worry. I am afraid that all you can do is to trust your daughter's good sense.

MAKE-UP

My daughter, Sally, has just turned eleven. All her interest, it seems, now centers on primping herself up, trying on all sorts of clothes, and wallowing in cosmetics. I think it is unseemly for a girl of her age to wear lipstick, but she claims we are persecuting her. I am afraid that with all this dolling up with false eyelashes and such, she will get in with the wrong kind of company. What do you say?

Don't be concerned about her getting into undesirable company, which I take means seducers and drug fiends. At her age, no adolescent group would accept her.

Maybe the girl feels she is plain or even ugly. Maybe, in fantasy, she identifies herself with some film star. I should not worry one bit about her; I'd give her as much in the way of cosmetics as she desired.

It sounds to me like she is an unhappy kid trying to escape from her unhappiness by pretending to herself that she is grown up. Is her school, is her home, too dull for her? Nagging her will only increase her dissatisfaction and make her hate her home and her parents. The girl feels unloved, feels she gets more criticism than appreciation, and she is now trying to win attention.

Mother, if you are just too worried, I suggest that you buy a stock of cosmetics, and deck your own face with thick goo, and put on the biggest false eyelashes you can buy. Then see what will happen.

Parents must remain young if they are to retain their children's love and understanding. Most parents gladly make sacrifices when the child is a baby; they accept the necessity of being kept awake, of hearing the infant's cries. But when the child grows older, the same parents conceive that they do not need to make any further sacrifices. At that stage, the youthful cry goes up: "You are behind the times."

A mother of a teenager might well ask herself: Do I ask my girl to do things that are unreasonable to her, like changing from her jeans to a frock because Mrs. Jones is coming to tea? Am I anxious when she goes out with a boy whom I don't know? Do I nag her about her school reports?

My suspicion is that your chief concern is what will the neighbors and relatives think. I say: To hell with what the neighbors and relatives think. If your girl develops into an unhappy adult, not one of those relatives or neighbors will give a damn, or bear your pain or the girl's pain. Half the kids in the world are sacrificed to neighbors' opinions.

I never see any girl in Summerhill—pupil or staff—use cosmetics. Is the deep answer that freedom consists in being able to live without having to consider what others think?

CLOTHES

Lucy Mae has taken to wearing short skirts, openwork stockings, bikini type separates and every other kind of dress that repels me. I am worried stiff about her attracting the fast type. I am a 39-year-old widow, and she is 16.

The girl, I am sad to say, has had precious little home life, for her father died when she was two and I have had to support the family since. I am deadly worried about her future and what direction she seems to be going. To all my remonstrances she says I am old-fashioned and don't know the styles.

By *fast type* you mean the type that will seduce your girl, but someone once said that in seduction it takes two.

Your real fear is a fear of sex. It may be but small consolation to you when I suggest that men are not attracted by bikinis or by openwork stockings, but by faces and by figures. Your daughter seeks to make herself attractive to men—just as her mother must have done before her.

Parents must realize that they have no ultimate control of their children, that the children must live their own lives in their own way. Millions of young girls dress in a "fast" way, but that does not necessarily mean they are promiscuous in sex.

We adults have got to tolerate the costumes of the new generation. To me leather jackets and tapered jeans appear to be feeble things, but I accept them just as I accept the noises the young call music. For all I know, you have too long chosen your daughter's dresses, and if so, the dresses now chosen by her are by way of protest. I advise leaving the lass alone. Let her make her own choices, both in dress and in life.

You are disturbed about superficialities. Assume, for the moment, that your son was a sadist or an arsonist. Assume that you had to write and tell me that your daughter was a shoplifter, or a prostitute, or a lesbian. Then worry would be called for. But worry over open-stockings and radically styled bathing suits? *Really!* I know how difficult it is for most elders to tolerate the behavior of their juniors, to accept their pop music, their long hair, their bosom-depicting sweaters, and all the rest. To us, the Beatle craze is a teenage neurosis; but to the young, it is a delight. We are out of touch.

'Twas ever thus. In each generation, the staid adults believe the young have lost respect, ideals and goals. In an Egyptian tomb, a stone was deciphered on which some pious old man of the Nile bemoaned—yes! this was 5,000 years ago—the waywardness of the young nihilists of his day. Youth, he wailed, was going to the dogs!

All the more reason for us to endeavor to understand the young, not to raise our hands in horror, nor to cry that the new generation is degenerate. I have half a mind to let my grey white hair grow to ten inches (and not because a Bond Street hairdresser offered to give me ten pounds for it, if I did).

I say let the young dress as they want to dress—and hands off!

My son has just come home from college where he's been a freshman for the last six months. We can hardly recognize him—his hair is long and unkempt, his clothes bedraggled. When we mention these facts, he goes off scowling saying we are interfering with his freedom. What is your opinion?

You *are* interfering with his freedom.

Is it the old story of what the silly neighbors think? Or have you a complex about order and cleanliness? Millions of children and young men and women suffer from parental anxiety about the trivial. The world is full of youths with long and unkempt hair and I cry: What the hell, anyway?

You should be more concerned about what is *under* his hair—what is he thinking about? What is he *feeling?*

I hate this eternal parental anxiety about the trifling things in life, the little things, the outward things. A balanced person is not overly concerned with inconsequential things like clothes and hair. I don't think that any of the many visitors that come to Summerhill ever notice that I do not wear a tie, or that I may need a shave. They come, interested in my educational methods; they do not come as reporters for the Tailor and Cutter Journal. And that should be the attitude of a parent to his child, a full regard for the personality—not for the fashion or lack of fashion.

MONEY

My boy of 13 is a pretty nice boy, but apparently is improvident. He always seems to be squandering his pocket money. We don't mind this so much, because we feel that this kind of money is meant to be disposed of on impulse.

But David has been given fairly good sums of money by relatives as Christmas gifts, birthday gifts, etc., and he has never seemed to buy a single thing that was useful or that lasted any length of time. He hasn't ever saved a penny. He takes $15 or $20, goes down to the store, and on a whim picks up some trash which he tires of in a week

**or less. Is there anything we can do to bring him into focus
with reality?**

I can't think of a thing, folks. Yours is a universal problem in an acquisitive society. In my own boyhood long long
ago, we got no pocket money. If we earned a penny, it was
for holding a farmer's horse while he had a pint in the local.
It was a long hold more than once. Middle and working
class children in those years simply had not the means to
spend, and therefore, not the temptation. We have got to
face the fact that we are living in a new world, a world in
which things come too easy to the children. "Easy come;
easy go!"

Today, children view pocket money as a right, a parental duty. I see the spending compulsion in youth everywhere. When I was a student and poor, I was lucky enough
to win £40 in a newspaper competition, an overwhelming
sum in 1910. That prize money kept me in clothes all my
undergraduate days. During the same period, a student pal
was left £50 by an uncle. He blew it all in one champagne
party. Modern youth appears to have his psychology.

The deep cause of your son's spendthriftiness may be
the state of this uncertain and unsafe world. *"Let us eat,
drink, and be merry, for tomorrow we die."* Youth will not
think of tomorrow, for youth feels there may not be a tomorrow. I fancy that every young man in U.S.A. has the deep
feeling when he reads the Vietnam casualty list: *"This
might be my future, or rather the lack of it."* The old safe
world has gone. Even money isn't very safe anymore.

After the first World War, folks in Germany who had
saved 100,000 marks over a lifetime found that the value of
their hard-won savings was worth but ten pfennigs. In 1919,

I paid about half a million marks for a tram ride. Our old values have had to be scrapped. In England, we once used the phrase: *Safe as houses,* but we dropped that simile after the blitz.

I am convinced that our education is at the root of spending. Spending is almost completely uncreative—unless we buy a tool set or a set of paints. The schooling of today is almost wholly uncreative and uninteresting. Youth seldom buys music scores, or canvases, or easels, or saws, or planes, because most schools barely touch making and doing. It is an age of looking on, of paying professionals to entertain us in music, in plays, in TV, in games. Hence an uncreative youth seeks happiness in gadgets like cars, motor bikes, pop records. The Beatles would have fallen flat in a society that was creative.

I know all this is not helping you worried parents of David. Your only consolation should lie in the thought that time itself may change the lad's values. Certainly advice and moral lectures will not help.

I, too, have pupils in my school who get too much money. Most of them do what David does—squander it. They themselves don't think they are misspending.

Money can have a symbolic meaning, obvious in the case of an unloved child whose parents over-compensate for their lack of love by showering expensive presents on their youngster. For all I know, David may feel he isn't loved at home; obviously his buying and then losing interest in the purchase shows he is seeking something by buying, something that the possession cannot satisfy.

Parents, you will simply have to grin and bear it. Just remember that nagging the boy will only make things worse.

RESTRICTIONS

I am 14. My parents are very strict and will never let me do what I want to. They forbid my boy friends from coming to the house. What can I do?

I think I have had at least 50 letters from American adolescents in this strain. Well, what *can* you do? Who can make your parents realize that they are unwittingly converting your love into unconscious hate?

Every second American I meet seems to be in therapy; and to judge from the mail I get from boys and girls, I am not surprised. So many American adolescents feel themselves coffined by parental taboos and demands. *"You must study and go to college, or you won't get a good job."* Unfortunately, American freedom, granted to the slaves in 1865, was never extended to the ordinary American child.

DEFIANCE

I am utterly dismayed because my daughter of 14 is so unfeeling. At her age, I would expect a child to have some concern for her mother who has loved her for many years and has given all her best to her. Although we get on outwardly, she does not communicate with me in the true sense of the word. I sense overwhelming narcissism. She does not care a hoot about my feelings, or what happens to me or her brothers and sisters. Do you think that a child is born with lack of feeling, or do you think something happened within the family that made her turn out this way? Is there any hope?

There is always hope.

In any family, there comes a stage in a child's life when she has to untie the family apron strings. The situation is, of course, worse in an authoritarian family. Self-regulated children do not have so much necessity to break away. In this case, it does not mean that the girl has no feeling; it means that all her feeling has turned negative.

But why? Have you, her parents, bound her with hoops of steel? Have you lectured her, "*You should be an example to your brothers and sisters?*"

Lack of feeling? I am inclined to think that the cause is environmental rather than hereditary. I suspect your daughter feels she has not been loved enough; perhaps she fancies that some of the other children have had more mother love than she has had. There *is* hope, but only if you, her mother, do something to change YOUR attitude.

I have had girls who have come to Summerhill with hate in their faces. They were impossible at home. Yet they all changed. It was a delight to see how their faces altered and showed tenderness. I gave them no therapy; I only stood back and allowed them to be their true selves. Gradually, their bitchiness disappeared.

The same result can be achieved at home if a girl feels she is free to be herself without nagging or criticism or lecturing.

But if the parents are not inwardly free enough, they will not succeed. The parents have, first of all, to be convinced that their former ways were wrong. In the newly given freedom, they must act wholeheartedly, without reservation, and unplagued by doubt. The girl must feel that she is not the subject of an experiment, but that her parents' attitudes have fundamentally changed forever.

**My daughter is 14 and unusually hostile to me. I haven't
any idea why. My wife agrees that I have always treated
her with kindness and consideration. Can you offer any advice to a baffled father?**

Most every child seeks at one time or another to break
the emotional chains which bind him to his parents. Most
children have some sort of shame about their parents. A girl
may be ashamed of her father—he spits on the street, he
makes a noise with his soup, he says things in company that
embarrass her. Most children grow out of the shame stage;
and most children in the end get over their annoyance with
the backward parent.

Try to relax and try not to impose your personality or
your viewpoints on your daughter. Had I a daughter in a
rebellious, faultfinding stage I would refrain from saying
to her anything other than little things—*Pass the salt, please.*

One feature may be important: whether it be conscious
or unconscious, nothing dies in a child's memory. The girl
may be reacting to things that you said or did when she was
four. Nothing can be done about this; the past is past. Yet
a parent can profitably ask himself: Was I too demanding,
too strict, too frightening when she was a baby?

There are other aspects, too. Do you and your wife
quarrel? Has love flown from the home? Does this lassie
feel that things are not right between her parents? Is she on
the side of her mother—against her father? Or has she so
strong a fixation on you, that to over-compensate, she has to
express hate instead of the love she is suppressing? A fair
guess is that your girl feels that you do not love her deeply
enough, and that your consideration for her feelings is only
a substitute for love.

In any case, leave her be. She will probably work out of it in time.

My son, Bob, is 17. He seems to resent his home. He never tells us a thing about what he is doing. If he comes home at two A.M., and I ask him where he has been, he just scowls and grunts. My husband and I feel that we have lost him.

I fear you have, good lady, but you lost him years ago. Both you and your husband failed to make contact with him, failed to make him feel he could trust you.

I suspect that he has lied to you all the way. "*Where were you tonight?*" Son has been out with a dame, but he cannot tell his parents that—so he lies. "*I went to the movies with Jim.*"

Children always lie to "bad" parents, to parents who have tried to fashion their children, to parents who teach them manners and behavior and obedience and what not. In Britain, about 25 adolescent girls run away from home each week and are not traced.

My dear lady, it is too late.

Was your boy beaten, or raged at, or circumscribed by all sorts of moral taboos? Did you force him to be religious?

But do not blame yourself too much. You believed you acted for the best; you naively thought that experience can be handed on from the old to the young. It cannot! Your own parents, maybe, kept you at arm's length, treated you as something to be shaped by the parental potter's hands. You survived; but every child does not take kindly to being spun on the potter's wheel.

Anyhow, cheer up! It does not mean the end of the

world—either for you or for your son. Many a lad has been reticent with his parents; many a lad has lied to them stoutly; all such boys did not end up as gangsters or dope fiends. It looks to me as if your son is now trying to fashion his own life. In your place, I should not interfere. I should cease to ask him where he has been, or what he has been doing.

To his father I say: Try to get in touch with your son emotionally. Drop being the heavy father. You can try to make him your chum—even at this late date. *Yes, your chum!* If you condemn him and lecture him, you will lose him forever. Why not try a way that is different than your old way. At this point, you've nothing to lose. It may be cruel to say it, but I make the guess that the lad has been starved for love at home and now seeks love elsewhere.

INTERMARRIAGE

I have fallen in love with a Catholic boy and want to marry him. In order to do so, I must agree that our children will be reared as Catholics. I hate the idea. What can I do?

If your hate of all indoctrination of children is not very strong, you will marry your young man. If you are prepared to have your children educated to believe that they are born in sin, you will marry your Catholic.

It really is a cruel dilemma. Love is instant; it lives for the day. Children, at this stage of the game, are only an idea in your life—an idea that is some distance away in time.

No advice. You will finally follow whichever of your feelings are the stronger.

Family Tension

PARENTAL DISAGREEMENT

My husband is fearfully impatient with the children. If they don't respond exactly the way he thinks they should and he expects them to, he just stands up and rails. The usual burst starts with "When I was a boy, if I did that, my father . . ." I have told my husband again and again that he lacks tolerance and that he is having a bad effect on the children. He is filling them with fear. He just doesn't listen. Worse, he is confirmed in his attitudes. Outside of this very rigid concept of obedience and right and duty, he makes a good husband. He loves me; he loves the children. He supports the family, and he acts intelligently in most matters. I do not want to divorce him, but I am at my wit's end as to what to do. Convincing him to be more gentle with the children seems to be hopeless. Shall I talk to my children and tell them that I disagree with their father's attitude? Or what?

A sad case this—and alas! a very common one.

No thinking man will ever use the futile words: "When I was your age." A genuine fully alive man would ask himself what *he* was at their age. Then, stripping away the humbug and the self-deception, he would be bound to conclude that in youth he was exactly like his children—rebellious, lying, what not.

Your husband seems to be identifying with his own stern father; he is thus continuing the vicious circle of hate; and poor fellow, just as he was conditioned, so is he automatically conditioning *his* family.

What surprises me in your question is your statement that "He loves me; he loves the children." How can love and authority live side by side? How can love live with fear? A man who puts his theories of discipline before his true duty to his children cannot really love them—that is, if we define love as giving out warmth.

What can you do? You ask if you should tell your children about the disagreement. I don't know their ages but you need not tell them; they have long ago grasped the situation—emotionally, if not intellectually. And these poor kids will suffer all their lives from an atmosphere that lacks real love and security.

One cannot dogmatize about the advantages or the disadvantages of a divorce. More than once I have seen children become happier after a divorce; the eternal depressive atmosphere of the strained home ceases. The best results are where the parents part sensibly without hate or anger, and where the children spend holidays with each in turn. The bad cases are those where one parent tries to influence the children against the other. That is very bad. When love dies, it is sheer tragedy when outright hate takes its place.

I cannot think of a solution for you or for the thousands of mothers in your predicament. Heavy fathers are always bad fathers; any father or teacher who arouses fear is a danger to young life.

One of the curses of humanity is that marriage begins with sexual love or romantic love or both. When love dies, as often as not life becomes hell. Love is blind, they say, and it is true. A Protestant woman may fall in love with a Catholic, and her passion drowns any still small voice in her about the future of her children. But when the primary passion has become moribund, she has to face the fact that she has pledged her children to be reared in his faith—in a faith that she doesn't believe in. And then there's hell to pay.

And so it is in other aspects. Passionate love rules out the proper questions: *Is he going to be a stern father? Will he make the children afraid? Is he determined to mold them in his own image? Is he to take as his parental motto: Children should be seen and not heard?* Tens of thousands of unhappy marriages result from the inability of one partner to know what the other really is. In courting, we put our best apples on the top of the barrel—not deliberately, just unconsciously.

One possible solution would be Judge Lindsay's companionate marriage. Make the first year a testing time; then marry if the couple finds unison, if the two would-be-partners find out for sure that they both feel the same way about life and about children.

Marriage as an institution is faulty. It postulates that you fall in love at 20, and remain in love till "death do us part." Millions of children are wretched because of the unhappy marriages of their parents.

In our day, cases such as yours remain insoluble; men and women just go on suffering. Strindberg's *Totentanz* presented a grim picture of a marriage that was one of hate; unfortunately, the marriage that is the dance of death goes on in so many homes.

My husband and I have, I suppose, as many disagreements as most couples—no more, no less. At times the quarrels become acrimonious. It is true that these times are rare, but when they do happen my husband lets off steam without restraint in front of the children. I upbraid him privately and tell him that no matter what the merits of his case happen to be, he has no right to explode in front of the family. I think that has a very harmful effect on the children.

He, on the other hand, says that he is not a machine and that when he feels very intensely he must react or else he is untrue to himself. He says that if he didn't explode when he felt he must, the anger would seethe below the surface and things between us, as husband and wife, would be much worse. With whom would you agree?

If your husband did not explode I fancy that the children would sense the strained atmosphere anyway. Maybe it is better if he lets off steam publicly. Why he has to do so I do not know, but I suspect that some of the steam should have been let off in his office or shop or wherever he works. The snag is that letting off steam seldom helps the angry one, often because the steam should have been blown somewhere else. A man is told off by his boss; he dare not reply with anger. He goes home and explodes over some silly little thing . . . the cat has messed in the living-room corner, or the supper isn't ready.

One unfortunate aspect of parental quarrels is that the children are almost forced to take sides. If the father is a frightening man with a roaring voice, the children will unconsciously side with the frightened mother. If the mother screams at the husband, he naturally evokes sympathy. In either case, it is all very upsetting. But I don't know what can be done about it.

In a situation which has progressed to sheer, unbridled acrimony constantly repeated, it would be better to break up the home than to have the children grow up in an atmosphere of hate and fear. Obviously, this is not the case here.

I have a daughter of seven. I believe in self-regulation but my husband says that a child must be disciplined and, when necessary, punished. What is the solution to my problem?

I wish I knew. You might agree to separate, and in that case the court might give your husband the custody of the child. It is a situation that appears in thousands of homes. In a home like yours, your daughter must be unhappy and insecure. *Who is right, Mommy or Daddy?*

Such a situation can never be hidden from the child; even if you do all your quarrelling in private, the child will sense the strain, the misery, the hostility.

I have had scores of letters like this. In most cases the fathers were the disciplinarians. Many of the letters have come from the children themselves who were aware of the parental conflict, pathetic letters to read.

One damnable thing about marriage is that the blindness of love makes the lovers unaware of all potential difficulties. We see this in the case of a girl who marries a Catholic, knowing but ignoring the fact that she will have to agree to the children being raised in the Catholic faith. When her romantic love dies, she may have to face a bitter situation, and she may feel powerless and wretched. Nor can a young woman always know that her young husband will turn out to be a sadist or an ugly authoritarian.

Or on the other side of the coin, the sweet little darling wife may turn out to be a shrew who nags the whole day long—a slapper of young children. This is all platitudinous, of course. Everyone knows the situations that arise. What many do not know is the appalling result in frightened, miserable, loveless children—children, who in their turn, will tend to unhappy marriages and continue the vicious circle, disciplining their own children.

Unless a child feels secure, he is doomed to a neurotic life. He may unconsciously try to reproduce the home situation everywhere he goes. He will unconsciously seek unhappiness. I find that the homesick child in my school comes from a bad home, a divided home. In his short lifetime, he has known much bickering, much fear, and much misery. In some obscure way, he wants to return to it all, no doubt fearing to be away from an environment, which no matter how awful, is at least familiar. One small boy told me that he wanted to go home because he wanted to protect his mother when his father hit her.

When a parent makes his child afraid, he is sinning against the child. I cannot see any connection between discipline and love. Some Catholics who beat their children at home and in school claim that they beat the body to save the soul, a claim that to me is totally anti-Christian. "Suffer the little children to come unto Me"—and get a hiding!—a clever combination of the loving Jesus and the foolish Solomon. Arbitrary commands are wrong, dangerous, and without love for the child.

Children throughout the world are being perverted by insane treatment. The bully in a school is often so stupid that he can retort to a supposed insult only with his fists, and it may be so in many homes.

Beating is more common among uneducated people than among the educated, but we all know of doctors and teachers and lawyers and businessmen who are stern with their families.

A few years ago in England two delinquent brothers were addressed by the judge. "If your father had given you both a good hiding every time you were behaving badly, you would not now be standing in the dock." It was later revealed that the father, an ex-army sergeant, had beaten them severely all the way from babyhood.

Brutality and superstition seem to have an affinity for each other. But one does not need to hit to make a child afraid. There is little or no corporal punishment in most American schools, but hundreds of teachers in the United States make children tremble by raging at them. The whole question boils down to hate. Unless we can solve the awful question of what breeds hate, people will go on for generations trying to compensate for a youth of frustration and unhappiness. Kill love of life in a baby, surround teenagers with all sorts of warning, and there will be a steady stream of recruits for the army of delinquency.

I'm sorry I cannot help you. Your husband's need to discipline and punish your child is an expression of his hate and will only produce hate in her.

I want to send my daughter to Summerhill but my husband is dead against it. Luckily I have a private income and will pay the fees myself. Will you take her?

Sorry, the answer is no. Summerhill would not help her. During every vacation, she would have to face the fact that her parents were divided about her education; she would not know where she stood. *Stood* is the word, for she would stand still.

If home and school are at odds, there can be no progress. No child should be asked to choose between two systems; freedom, like peace, is indivisible.

GRANDPARENTS

My husband's mother lives with us. Being of a different generation, she does not share our ideas about child rearing. She constantly tells our little girl not to do this and not to do that, urges her to eat this and that, and otherwise interferes with the atmosphere of the home. We are at our wits' end as to what to do with our little Sally. We cannot turn grandmother out. Have you any advice?

What can I say? A child is being sacrificed to the dead ideas of an old woman. Yet the old lady cannot be turned out. It is hopeless to try to get her to change her thinking.

I can see no solution for you as parents, and little help for Sally who must be in conflict. The child must say to herself, *"Mommy and Daddy let me do this, but Granny says it is wrong."*

The only hopeful factor is that the child is bound to prefer the free attitude of her parents rather than the anti-life attitude of grandma.

BROKEN HOME

My husband has left home. We had not been getting on, and this rupture was a final step in a series of altercations. Our boy was very close to his father who, in my opinion, overcoddled him. Now I am afraid that the boy will feel that he has been abandoned by the one male he was attached to. He loves me very much, but clearly, I am no father substitute. What can I do to lessen the blow to the boy?

You should take your child into your confidence. Don't

say, "Daddy is away all the time because he has to work in Chicago." Tell the truth. "Your Daddy and I don't love each other any more, so we agreed to part."

If you happen to be right that your husband over-coddled the boy, your lad may develop a grudge against you. He may think: "*If Mother had been good to Father, he wouldn't have gone away.*"

The situation will prove worse if the coddling was made a subject of dispute between you and your husband. Your son may feel that you have been attacking both him and his father. But I don't think that your husband's departure in itself is the center of the problem. For years, the boy must have sensed the growing gulf between his parents; the home could not have been a happy home for him.

One solution would be for the boy to live part time with his father and part time with you. I have often had pupils who split up their vacations in this way, and it usually turned out to be satisfactory—at least, a partial solution.

Your remarriage will not of itself solve the problem. Many boys never take to a step-father, nor do many girls; it is always a risk. I'm afraid there's no pat solution.

SIBLING RIVALRY

Last night, I proposed to the family that we eat in a restaurant. My daughter, age eight, wanted to go to a Chinese place. My son, six, wanted to go to a delicatessen. Neither my husband nor I had any special preference: either restaurant would do. When I told the girl that we would make Johnny happy if we went to a delicatessen, she pouted and said, "Why should he get *his* way?" Then, when I tried to switch to a Chinese restaurant, the boy said, "Why should she get *her* way?" How do you reconcile a situation like this?

Why not make it a sporting event and toss for it?

The other day I saw two boys of seven quarreling about a comic they had found.

"I picked it up!" said one.

"Yes, but I saw it first," said the other.

I spun a penny. Heads, you; tails, you. They accepted the result quietly.

This sort of difference occurs almost daily in any family of young children. For my part I'd simply say: "Chinese tonight; but next time, a delicatessen." Every child has to become accustomed to a *No*. All those who voted for Goldwater had to accept the national *No*.

In every family, there is this question: Does Mommy favor Mary? In every family, there is much buried hate—engendered because one of the children feels that he has been misused, treated unfairly. The Spiritualists make a bad mistake when at their seances they say that your family is waiting on the blessed shore to welcome you.

Children have an uncanny sense of true justice. Toss that penny or dime.

We are a family of six. There are the usual squabbles between the children, but Joan seems to attract more than the usual quota to her corner. If there's a fight at home, the chances are three to one that she's in it. How can it be that this one child out of six finds it more difficult than the other five to get along with her peers?

I don't know. She may think that she is the least loved of the batch. She may have a drive in her that makes her impatient. I simply cannot give an opinion on the bare facts.

I have two children. Mary is five and her brother, Donald, is three. At times, for no apparent reason, Mary will go over to Donald and just strike him. The little boy breaks out crying. It is pitiful to see him. How can I handle this baffling situation?

Two years ago, I had a letter from a young mother in Boston who was confronted with precisely the same situation you find yourself in. Her family and yours coincided in every detail. Her children were the same ages as yours, and the girl was the elder of the two.

When her daughter of five struck her three-year-old brother, that wise mother made it a practice to pick up the little boy, cuddle him, and soothe away his tears. She never upbraided the girl. She never even remonstrated, but in a voice as mild as she could command she directed her little daughter to play with her dishes or to get occupied with something else.

Her last letter runs as follows: "My little boy is now seven. He is very much attached to his sister and she, in turn, is very much attached to him. They play together quite peacefully and are each concerned about how the other is doing and how the other feels. The element of sibling rivalry has obviously diminished. I don't doubt that that factor still exists, but I see an abatement of aggression on her part and an attitude on the boy's part that implies he has forgotten the assaults she once perpetrated on him."

There is a smart mother. She handled the matter in the only way such a situation can be handled. She knew, with profound sense, that the roots of her daughter's unprovoked aggressions lay in sibling rivalry. That mother knew that scolding wouldn't help. She understood that if she punished the little girl it would only deepen the unconscious resentment the child felt against her brother, the boy who had come into the family and who had caused a lessening of that little girl's importance.

In Summerhill, not too long ago a small boy had a row with another child. The little tyke felt that he had lost the battle, so he gathered a few bricks and expended his rage by breaking 12 windows. His young housemother came to me and asked if the boy should be charged at a general meeting of the school and a punishment exacted. I said no. I told her to take the boy on her knee and cuddle him and never mention the word "window." The housemother took my advice, and in this way the boy's anger was diminished. Maybe his young rival had fought with him and didn't love him, but surely here was an adult who cherished him.

Jealousy in a family is common. One of the most difficult tasks of a parent is to steer clear of the accusation of favoritism. Almost every child formulates the question: "Does mother love me as much as she loves my sister Mary?" It is my observation that in a home where the parents are placid, the children are likely to get along together without too much strife. Children are imitative. If father rages against mother, or father rages against them, they will be inclined to bully their juniors. If mother is a nagger, the child is likely to be a nagger.

Parents should be especially wary about comparing one child with another: *"Your brother, George, never pulls the cat's tail."* "*Why can't you sit still and read quietly like your sister, Sue?*" Wise parents never make odious comparisons of that kind.

ADOPTION

Should we tell our child that we are his adopted parents?

Yes, of course. If your child has known your love since infancy, you have little to fear. Most adopted children were unwanted by their real mothers. Every child psychologist knows the sad consequences when a baby gets no love. In a long career, I have found that the children I could not do very much for were those who had never been loved as babies. Such poor kids go through life with a suspicion, a feeling of inferiority, a fear of emotional contact. Freedom can ameliorate that starved emotional state, but freedom cannot completely cure the damage. The adopted child who is a problem child is not really protesting against his foster parents; he is going farther back—*feeling*, not thinking—"*I was never wanted by my mother. She left me, and I hate her forever.*"

Some of my pupils who have been adopted have tried to meet their natural mothers to re-establish a relationship; the experiment has never been successful. The mother that was met was a stranger, not the warm, embracing mother of their infant dreams. I am a little bit nervous about adoption.

An adopted child must be told the truth, no matter how old he was when adopted. If you tell a girl of six that she is adopted, with good loving parents she is likely to forget the fact—if her parents are good and loving; if you suppress the information, the shock of later discovery may have serious results. Some foster parents think: *The baby was adopted when she was six weeks old. She cannot possibly ever know about it. No need to tell her.* That path can be dangerous, for children have ways and means of ferreting out secrets. I knew one boy who discovered the truth when he was 16. His foster parents told me that after that shock he had become cool and secretive in his relations with them. Safest to tell the truth.

It is because I fear for the future of rejected children that I am all for legal abortion. Abortion is far less harmful to society than a hating child. It is a scandal that our anti-abortion laws were made by men. Only a plebiscite of women, both married and single, should determine whether abortion is to continue to be a punishable crime. Alas, women, too, have been molded; I fear that the majority of women might also be against abortion.

When parents who have their own children adopt another, there may still be a danger. Given the intense jealousies in the ordinary family, what happens when a child of five is suddenly introduced into an intimate group of other children of seven and ten? What must be the conflicting emotions among the children who now have to share the parental love and attention with an interloper?

A similar situation arises in a boarding school where a married teacher comes with his own child. More than once I have had to ask a married teacher to leave because his own child was becoming a problem. *"I had Mommy and Daddy all to myself; now they give all their time to 50 other kids."*

My advice to teachers and housemothers: never have

your children in the school you teach in. I was a pupil in my father's village school and I got leathered more violently than the other boys, partly because my father did not want to show any favoritism, party because he was angry that his son did not set a good example in behavior and studies.

There is something uncanny about a child; he almost seems to have a special sense. An illegitimate child does not know he is a bastard, but he *feels* there is some mystery about him. Similarly, parents who try to hide from their children the fact that they no longer love each other are astounded to learn that the child sees through it all, despite their attempt to disguise the situation by calling each other *Darling* or *Honey*. There is really very little that you can hide from children. In two separate instances I have known adolescent girls who were born a month before their parents' wedding. Their parents lied about their birth dates so that they did not know the fact itself, yet why did they go off to the Registry Office and ask to see their birth certificates? Must have been either a special sense, or some spiteful remark by someone who had heard the gossip. The moral is live the truth, and tell the truth.

PARENTAL ATTITUDE

Last night, my husband and I were about to go out for the evening. Our little youngster, age six, started to cry. He didn't want us to go, he said, because he didn't like the babysitter. The babysitter wasn't exactly a dreamboat in appearance nor an intellectual giant. She seemed sufficiently pleasant, but evidently had little imagination. We had a firm commitment with other people; in addition, we anticipated a good deal of pleasure from the evening. However, we were conscience-stricken about leaving the child crying. My husband and I have been talking this matter over and we are nonplussed. Can you offer any counsel?

Change the babysitter, of course. That does not solve the question of the moment—to go out with friends or to stay at home and comfort the baby. My wife and I agree that we would have cancelled the party and have stayed with the child; but the particular circumstances, I grant, may have made such a decision difficult, even though as parents, you couldn't really enjoy a night out when you knew that your youngster was screaming his head off.

Of course, some children will bully their parents by screaming when things don't go their way. On the other hand, this child may have had an idea that he was being left at home too often; the babysitter may have been to him a symbol of neglect, and the incident of the particular evening you write about may have been the climax in a situation that had been brewing for some time.

At best, a babysitter is an agent paid to let the parents have some external life of their own; she can never be a satisfactory substitute for the mother. Parents of young children have to sacrifice much—their sleep, their social life, their gadgets. Each couple must decide for themselves how far that sacrifice should go.

Therapy

FEAR

My son is a fearful child. He hesitates to try anything new. If he is not encouraged—sometimes even forced—to try things, whether they be ice-skating, new foods, or just sitting tranquilly at home with a baby-sitter, how will he ever overcome his fears and gain confidence in himself?

Why ice-skating or new foods? Why *should* he choose them? I have had boys in my school for 12 years who never once kicked a ball or played tennis.

The fact that the boy fears to stay home with a new baby-sitter suggests that he has too strong a dependence on his parents. Probably behind his fear is the unconscious anxiety that they will not return. The facts as stated suggest that you want to mold your boy, to tell him how to live, what to do, what to eat. No child should ever be forced to eat what he does not want to eat. No child should be prompted to go ice-skating unless he desires to do so.

I can say nothing about his fears. I would suggest consulting a good psychologist. So many things might have happened. You may not have wanted to bear him; his father may be a stern disciplinarian; he may be overshadowed by an extroverted brother or sister. The general atmosphere of the home may account for a lot that is under the surface.

Two years ago, a new pupil came to Summerhill, a boy who was so timid and scared of everyone that he literally spoke in a whisper. Last night, I opened my office door and shouted to that boy, "Tom, stop that infernal row. I can't talk to my visitor." With the changed atmosphere, the fear in that boy's psyche has disappeared.

Janet is 12 and fears water, even in a shallow pool. I feel she should learn to swim. As I have no success through persuasion, is there anything I can do to remedy the situation?

Yes, if you can afford it, get a therapist to try to see why she has a phobia of water. On no account try to persuade her to swim; that will make her phobia much worse.

There may be a known origin. To be personal for a moment: my grandfather was drowned. When we were small, my grandmother would stand on the beach and yell to us: "Don't go out any farther, or you'll be drowned." All of us children got a complex about drowning. It took a lot of therapy for me to overcome the fear of water. Had I been forcibly thrown into a pool to sink or swim, I might well have become a more hopeless neurotic than I am.

I have had children in my school who used to fear water; nearly all gradually overcame their fears and became good swimmers.

So, parents, no suggestion, no forcing, and worst of all no cry of coward.

Why are some children timid and fearful—almost, it would seem from birth?

I have no idea. Since the study of psychology is just barely developing, we simply do not know very much about the human personality. In the very same family, one child is an extrovert, the other an introvert. Why? We know little or nothing about pre-natal influence.

Maybe a timid child stems from an anxiety stage of the mother while she was carrying the baby. Even if this guess were established as a fact, how could we prevent the birth of a timid child? Who knows if loud noises affect the child in the womb? Who knows whether a child is fearful because his mother did not want to have him? I can offer nothing in answer to your question.

STUTTERING

My boy stutters. Neither my husband nor I understand why. Do you?

I don't. I can only make the guess that he is trying to screen his personality, for I have never had a stuttering pupil who stuttered when acting in a play where he took on a different personality.

I have no idea how stuttering can be cured, but I believe a speech therapist might help.

PSYCHOTHERAPY

Should children have psychotherapy?

This is a question about which authorities differ profoundly. Here are my own opinions for what they are worth.

I used analysis for many years with children; later, I began to doubt if that procedure was necessary. An adult who feels neurotic *voluntarily* undertakes therapy; no child ever does. This is not to say that the children I treated did not get something out of the analysis—they did. Everyone, whether old or young, likes to have someone he can talk to about himself.

Listening to a disturbed child is an act of love. That may be the reason why so much therapy succeeds. I used to wonder why one man would be analyzed by a Freudian, another by a Jungian, another by an Adlerian, and each and every patient improved. Was it the feeling each got that the therapist was giving him the love each had sought from his own father or mother?

I doubt whether the uncovering of infantile memories is as important as the analysts claim it is. Certainly the making conscious of the cause of a complex does not in itself cure that complex. If the uncovering of an infantile memory brings about the same emotional reaction as took place in the original trauma, then of course, the revelation may effect a cure. But too often, an explanation only changes the symptom. A man may suffer from headaches because his father always hit him on the head; making the origin of his headaches conscious may displace his complaints to lumbago.

There are thousands of psychotherapists in private practices treating, for the most part, people who can afford the time and the money. If every therapist in the world were to do nothing but educate parents about child psychology, telling them primarily what *not* to do with their children, there would be little need for adult therapy of any kind. How many psychoanalysts have said: "Patching up adults isn't good enough. I'll devote my life to prophylaxis, and I'll begin with mothers and babies."

Getting back to the question: Nowadays, I put my trust in freedom. Freedom works in nearly all cases—although freedom is not entirely therapeutic with children who were starved for love as babies.

But don't ask me to precisely explain how freedom works a cure for I really don't know. At Summerhill, we once got a girl of 14 who had tried more than once to commit suicide. She came to us with a hard face, a bitter voice, a suspicious look. At our self-government meetings, she always voted to exonerate the anti-social offenders. After two years at Summerhill, she walked around with a relaxed body and a happy face. Exactly why, I cannot tell. I can only suggest that when a child is in an approving environment without anyone's telling her how to behave and how to live, the good side automatically comes out. I could cite many other instances of similar results.

Freedom is supported not by talking, but by doing. The best way to cure a boy who wants to smash windows is to laugh and help him break the panes. Not so easy I admit, if the parents of the boy are poor. I have had to stand by and see an adolescent boy damage my precision lathe, knowing that if I interfered he would identify me with his military father who would never allow him to enter his workshop.

Being on the side of the child is the best therapy. I confess my ignorance of the child clinics that do fine work with play therapy, but I cannot see the point in Melanie Klein's demand that every child should be analyzed at four years old.

A child brought up in freedom should not require any analysis at all.

I am a young teacher in a grade school in Kansas. I am presently in analysis. Would I be helping the children in my class psychologically if I tell them what the symbolism of their stories and pictures means?

My answer is one big Never. I know from my own experience the temptation a young teacher has to experiment with the little he knows.

Fifty years ago, I read a book on hypnotism and thought I should have a go at it I hypnotized a young woman. When she was asleep, I said to her: "In two minutes, you will wake up and ask me what I paid for my boots."

In two minutes, she woke up looking rather confused. "Sorry," she said, "I must have fallen asleep."

Then she sat silent for a little time. "Oh, Lord!" she cried suddenly, "When I went to town this morning, I quite forgot to get aspirin for Mother and I was in Boots', too." Boots is a big drugstore in London.

Then her eyes wandered to my feet, and remained fixed on my shoes. "I have sometimes wondered where you get those broad-toed boots," she said. "What did you pay for them?" I was elated with success.

Next time I put her to sleep, I said: "Multiply 3,576,-856 by 568." She woke up looking dreadful. "Oh, God, I've got a hell of a headache," she said. After that, I never attempted hypnotism again.

A girl in class paints a landscape: two tall trees standing apart at each side—one a pine, a father symbol—the other a spreading chestnut, a mother symbol. Standing desolate in the center is a stunted tree—the girl. The picture symbolizes the girl's situation: parents who have ceased to love each other, unhappy parents who cannot give her enough love. But what point is there in giving that explanation to the child? It won't help. Worse, it might even kill her interest in art.

Now I'm not saying that if an analyst told Picasso the symbolism of his paintings, Picasso would give up art, for art is in the core of him. But that isn't true of everyone.

Fifty years ago, I knew a fellow student who was a very good boxer. When he went boxing at night, I always had to go with him because he was scared to walk the London streets late at night. He went to be psychoanalyzed. As a boxer, he had one bad fault that he knew about—he always dropped his hands. He mentioned this habit to his doctor. His analyst explained to him that unconsciously he was really trying to protect his genitals. . . . the good old castration complex. That lad never boxed again.

One of my little girls wrote a story about a father, a wicked witch (the mother), a beautiful young princess (herself). The father married the princess—an Oedipus plot if there ever was one. How dare anyone step in and interpret that story to the little girl. It would be shameful.

The old fallacy still lingers that making a complex conscious by explaining its origins cures the complex. *It does not!* I am against telling children the symbolism of anything they do or say. The interpretation of symbolism is always arbitrary. Is a snake a penis symbol? . . . . A bull, a father? Is a necktie a phallic symbol? Who can be sure? Carl Jung pointed out that Aladdin's lamp was phallic, for a man had only to rub it to get all the joys in the world.

I went through a short analysis with Wilhelm Stekel, one of the great authorities on symbolism; his dream analysis was fascinating, but how much did it help patients?

Stekel used to tell of a party he went to at an artist's studio. The talk turned to symbolism. Stekel gave his contribution, but his host would not have it. "Nonsense, Stekel, I don't accept a word of it." The artist pointed to a picture on the wall. "Mean to say there is symbolism in that still life I painted?"

Stekel put on his glasses. "Yes, there is."

"What sort of symbolism?"

"Ah," said Stekel, "I couldn't tell you in public."

"Nonsense," cried the artist, "We're all friends here. Out with it."

"All right. When you painted that picture, you had just seduced a servant girl; she became pregnant, and you were searching for an abortionist."

The artist went white. "My God!" he cried. The great symbolist had uncovered the truth.

I asked Stekel how he came to it.

"The picture portrayed a dining table. A bottle of port had spilled over—the blood—the abortion. A sausage on a plate looked exactly like a fetus." Just how he rang in the servant girl, I can't recollect.

Interpreting symbolism is like a crossword, a pleasant game. I feel sure that such interpretations have rarely helped the patient. I am told that nowadays many analysts no longer interpret dreams—what Sigmund Freud called the royal road to the unconscious.

However that may be, a teacher should never touch symbols. For one thing he lacks the professional training. If a teacher is going to use psychology, he should do so in action and not in words. Hugging a child will do much more for a youngster than interpreting his dreams.

I am not saying that teachers should not study psychology. Far too few do. Teachers seem to shy away from anything that has to do with the emotions, and psychology is primarily the study of the emotions.

Is creative activity a good means of treating a young neurotic? I mean music, painting, but especially dance.

More than forty years ago when I was a teacher in a school in Dresden, Germany, we had a division devoted only to eurythmics and the dance, for girls of 16 and up. We often had an evening of solo dances. But it dawned on me that so many of the girls chose a *Totentanz*, and I began to wonder why girls who expressed their emotions all day long in movement should choose a Dance of Death. That experience killed the belief I had previously held that movement was curative.

No, I don't think that dance, or art, or music are in themselves curative. I wonder how many of the girls taking part in an opera chorus or studying in an art school or in a music school are really relaxed. One must remember that there is no real freedom in most schools of music, art, or the dance; the girls are under strict discipline in these schools. I imagine that the wonderful Russian dancers must be drilled like soldiers. Perhaps the least disciplined are the art students who stand and paint.

Given freedom to live freely, all children will benefit from movement and rhythm. For years, I have seen children learn to dance—not by taking lessons in foxtrot, tango, or the twist—but by free expression, by inventing as they go along. Most of my pupils dance as most Negroes dance— with relaxation, invention, and rhythm. So let us have all the dance and art and music we can give to children—but without the drilling and the discipline and the formality.

What about drama? How much does acting release? Well, drama can have a surprising result. I've often had stammerers in my school; yet every time a stammerer acted in a play, he enunciated well and spoke fluently. I suppose the reason was that by taking on another personality, the stammerer became a normal child.

This suggests that an actor is a man who runs away from his true personality. And why not? Do we not all run away by losing ourselves in a play, or by reading a novel, or in living through a movie, or in getting drunk?

We are apt to think in compartments. We support a bill to retain hanging, and next Sunday we go to Communion. We are all guilty of this kind of split behavior; we all have our complexes. I was delighted to read in a book by Erich Fromm that Freud had to be in the station an hour early whenever the great man had to catch a train.

I am not enamored of school plays: little moral, sentimental stories which feature angels with wings or fairy godmothers. I have strong views against children acting Shakespeare. They just don't understand Shakespeare; it's a pretension.

In Summerhill, the boys and girls write their own plays, make up the costumes, build the scenery, and produce the plays. But the most exciting acting in the school is the spontaneous acting on Sunday nights. This kind of acting can be done in any school. I begin with simple situations. I suggest something like: *Gather flowers; Wheel a heavy barrow; Be a blind man crossing the road.* Then I go on to talking: *Ask a policeman the way; Telephone for the doctor and get the butcher by mistake.* One boy handled this assignment by carrying on a confused conversation about liver.

Perhaps the fun and wit are of as much value to the children as the acting. One result of this kind of acting is the complete absence of nervousness; the child has no lines to forget. But I fancy this kind of evening works best where children are free. A few public school teachers have told me it is difficult to get their pupils to lose their self-consciousness and to banish their fear of failing.

Yes, spur-of-the-moment acting is great fun; and I guess that just plain fun produces more relaxation and release than does formal dance training.

INTROVERSION

Frankie is 11. He reads all the time. He stays indoors and his complexion is sallow. He won't go out and play with the other boys. My husband applauds his intellectual interests, but I think the boy is becoming a recluse. What can I do about my husband and the boy?

Frankie seems to be between two fires. To which side does he lean? Apparently to that of the father. I do not know if your husband is overly ambitious for the boy, if he is a man who feels that a lack of education hampered him in his life and he is therefore determined that his son will suffer no such handicap. All I know is that to command an introverted boy to be an extrovert and to go out and play games is a bad mistake. If the boy is encouraged by his father to be a reader rather than a doer, I cannot see any solution.

Some years back, the son of a professor attended Summerhill. His mother wrote me saying that she was alarmed because the boy sat all day and night reading Plato and Plutarch. He was with us in Summerhill for a few years; the only literature I ever saw him read was comics. He is now a good scientist.

I advise you to do nothing. Despite the paternal coaching, your son Frankie may one day be the Open Golf Champion.

A Final Word

I am in my last year of college. I want to start a school on Summerhill lines. Have you any advice to give me?

Only Punch's advice to those about to marry—*don't!* Unless you are prepared to go through a plethora of difficulties, and have the guts to face them and overcome them —don't open a school.

Some few people are opening schools on Summerhill lines, trying to set out from where Summerhill is now, forgetting that we have had 45 years of trial and error. We had to discover slowly what we could do, and what we couldn't do. Any new school on freedom lines will have to face the fact that the first pupils sent to it will, most likely, be problem children that home and school couldn't handle. Even today, during a period when Summerhill does not solicit problem children, too many new pupils fall into this category. The parents do not usually tell us the whole story, fearing no doubt, that we may not accept their child. *"My boy isn't a problem; he just doesn't like his school."* In two weeks, we find out that Willie is a thief and a bully. Of course, we do not like to send him home once he is in the school, and so we must bear Willie until he becomes humanized.

You will get parents who believe in freedom—but only intellectually; unconsciously they'll be working against the school influence. You will be obliged to deal with parents who become jealous when they learn that their child is happier at your school than he was at home.

In some states, you will probably encounter difficulty

183

with the religionists and with the sex puritans and with the body haters. In other localities, you might encounter some authority that would prevent your opening a radical school, giving as his pretext the excuse that the premises are not suitable.

You will need money. When I brought my school home from Austria in 1924, I had but five pupils; three of them paid half fees, the other two paid no fees at all. However, we were situated in a seaside resort, and by turning the school into a boarding house during the summer holidays we managed to struggle through. But I recall looking into a shop window, and wondering if I could afford to buy a spade.

Get your fees in advance, or you will land in my misfortune of losing much money through bad debts. But, alas, you will be a fool as I have always been, keeping on the children of the non-payers, simply because you like the kids.

Above all, you dare not compromise in essentials, else your school is doomed to failure. Freedom is ALL OR NOTHING; you can't have freedom and guidance together—so never call your staff *counsellors*.

A recent book, *Crime, Punishment, and Cure,* by Sington and Playfair, is a survey of crime and its causes. A brilliant book, impartial and forward-looking, this treatise must make any reader wonder about our values in education.

I never recommend books on Experimental Psychology, a subject which seems to figure prominently in university teaching, for I cannot see how the study of what rats will do in certain circumstances has any bearing on child behavior. Condition rats and they will behave in abnormal ways, granted. But we already know that when children are conditioned they will cease to be natural children. I'd rather that the study of rats gave way to the study of the evil elements in child education.

I, myself, never appoint a teacher on the strength of his college degrees, for such status does not convince me that the man automatically knows enough about child nature. Instead of a course in Experimental Psychology, I'd far rather have the prospective teacher read Homer Lane's *Talks to Parents and Teachers,* and David Wills' *Throw Away the Rod.*

To me, so many books on education and psychology are so ponderous in style, and are so fearfully wordy. Why do most scholars avoid simplicity? Where an uneducated man would write a letter to his local paper complaining about the disturbance of his sleep by a cat concert on the backyard fence, a pedantic teacher might write protesting against a concatenation of raucous sounds emanating from feline wanderers in the night.

Also see that you, personally, are officially qualified. You must know your subjects and know how to teach. Being kind in the classroom is not enough; you must be competent. Furthermore, if you want to deal with children, you must be entrenched against the powers that be. I hated Anglo Saxon but knew that without it I could not get my M.A. Hons. degree—a degree I never use—but that degree protects me. No authority can step in and say: "You aren't qualified to be a schoolmaster." The exams are there; if you have the guts, you will take them in your stride.

Keep your opinions to yourself. I have known young Communists in factories who proclaimed their politics from the housetops. They were fired—not of course because of their politics, oh, no—the firm was just reducing its overhead. If you go around saying you are an atheist or a sex reformer, you are in danger. Wait until you are established, and then you can say what you like.

You are undoubtedly aware that a few men, men no wiser than we are, have the power to press the H button. Yet all of us, accustomed to infant stage control, sit quietly by and do nothing about that awful situation. Our training, too, restrains most of us from roaring our indignation at the barbarous criminal code, at the stupid learning we name education, at the spending of millions on arms in a world in which the majority is underfed. You are, as I said, undoubtedly aware of the kind of world we live in, but if you are starting a radical school, you'll have enough to cope with, so don't advertise your iconoclasm about everything. I am not asking you to be insincere, only guarded in this Establishment world of ours.

Study child psychology, but follow no authority. If you are an earnest and solemn sort of a guy, don't start a school. Once I said to a girl of 14 who was making a box: "You are using too many nails." She scowled at me; and right then and there I knew I had lost her, for during all her life people had been telling her what not to do. After that, in her eyes I was an authority figure. The only good way to learn child psychology is through experience—not reading books.

Another warning: Every young man who deals with girls should watch out for the neurotic adolescent, prone to projection. Patting a sexually disturbed girl on the head can make her fantasy that you have made sexual advances to her. In the days when I dealt almost exclusively with problem children, I always got in touch with the psychiatrist who had sent the girl to me, when I saw indications that she might project her sex complexes on to me.

If you are going to run a school, it would be best to get

married first. A teacher who has no sex life is always in danger of conceiving an unconscious fixation on a pretty girl of 15. This statement applies to teachers of both sexes.

Above all, understand that children are the same all over the world. They all seek happiness, freedom, love; they all want to play and play and play. Yet they are all avid to learn about things that interest them.

And don't make too many blueprints. Be willing to make changes as the evidence unfolds. Ossified organization is death to pioneering.

Which reminds me of the story of the young devil in hell who rushed to his master in great perturbation.

"Master! Master! Something awful has happened; they have discovered truth on earth!"

The Devil smiled. "That's all right, boy, I'll send someone up to organize it."

Index

Abortion, 49, 72, 75, 76, 168
Adolescence, 125-154
  clothes, 145-146
  cursing, 130-134
  defiance, 150-154
  drinking, 138-140
  driving a car, 134-135
  drug addiction, 140-143
  intermarriage, 154, 156, 159
  make-up, 143-144
  money, 147-149
  restrictions, 150
  smoking, 135-138
  staying out late, 125-130
Adoption, 167-169
Aggressiveness, 105-108, 111-112
Alcoholism, 138
Anti-life attitudes, 24, 27-44, 66, 76, 85, 86, 106, 129, 131
  conventionalism, 38-39
  discrimination, 41-44
  dishonesty, 39-41
  duty and responsibility, 30-35
  gratitude, 28-29
  manners, 27-30
  respect, 36-38
Anti-Semitism, 42, 43-44
Apartheid, 42, 84

Babysitters, 169-170
Bach, J. S., 80
Batman, 19

Bean, Orson, 26
Beating, 160-161. *See also* Spanking.
Beatles, The, 121, 126, 146, 149
Berkeley University, 141
Boasting, 111
Brave New World, 126
Broken homes, 162-163. *See also* Divorce.
Bullying and fighting, 105-108, 111-112

Calvin, John, 84
Calvinist Church of South Africa, 42, 84
Capone, Al, 14
Careers, 78-81
Cars, driving by adolescents, 134-135
Censorship, parental, 81-82
Chaplin, Charlie, 53
Character molding, 88-94
Childhood, problems of, 99-124, 169-170
  babysitters, 169-170
  boasting, 111
  bullying and fighting, 105-108, 111-112
  daydreaming, 124
  destructiveness, 102-105
  fantasy, 123-124
  food and eating, 117-119

lying, 108-112
sleep, 119-121
spanking, 99-102
stealing, 112-115
sulking, 115
television, 115-116
thumb-sucking, 119
toys, 121-123
Chores, 32-35
Circumcision, 67-68
Civil rights, 90
Clay, Cassius, 82
Cleanliness, 11, 22
Clothes, 145-146
Comics, 82, 111, 182
Contraceptives, 68-71
Conventionalism, 38-39
Coolidge, Calvin, 110
Crime, Punishment, and Cure,
    184
Cursing, 22, 130-134

Dance, as therapy, 179-180
Daydreaming, 124
Defiance, in adolescence, 150-154
Delinquency, 129-130, 161
Destructiveness, 102-105
Dictionary of Slang, 131
Disagreement, between parents,
    155-161
Discrimination, 41-44, 70, 91
Dishonesty, 39-41
Divorce, 40, 70, 72, 156-157,
    162-163
Dope, 140-143
Drama, as therapy, 182-183
Drinking, 138-140

Driving a car, 134-135
Drug addiction, 140-143
Duty, 30-35

Eating, problems in childhood,
    117-119
Einstein, Albert, 44
*Elegy Written in a Country
    Churchyard,* 132
Empire State Building, 124
Encyclopaedia Britannica, 116
Etiquette, 27-28. *See also*
    Manners.

Family tension, 155-170
    adoption, 167-169
    broken homes, 162-163
    disagreement between parents,
        155-161
    grandparents, 162
    jealousy, 166-167, 168
    parental attitude, 169-170
    sibling rivalry, 163-167
Fanny Hill, 82
Fantasy, 123-124
Fear, 69, 78-79, 102, 112, 156,
    160, 171-173
Femininity and masculinity,
    66-67
Fighting and bullying, 105-108,
    111-112
Food, 117-119
Freedom, defined, 7-8
Freud, Sigmund, 44, 178, 180
Fromm, Erich, 180

Gandhi, Mohandas K., 107

Golding, William, 105
Goldwater, Barry, 164
Graham, Billy, 26, 83, 84, 91
Grandparents, 36-37, 162
Gratitude, 28-29
Gray, Thomas, 132
Great Dictator, The (film), 53
Grimaldi, 52

Hardy, Thomas, 81
Harris, Frank, 8
Hate, 91, 161
Hitler, Adolf, 42, 53, 83, 107
Homework, 60-61
Homosexuality, 49, 71-73
Humor, importance of, 51-53
Huxley, Aldous, 126
Hypnotism, 176

Incest, 25
Influencing children, 75-97
    about careers, 78-81
    censorship, 81-82
    character molding, 88-94
    marriage, 94-97
    religion, 84-88
    undesirable companions, 83
Intermarriage, 94-96, 154, 156, 159
Introversion, 181-182
Ivanhoe, 116

Jealousy, 166-167, 168
Jesus, 84, 85, 87, 108, 160
Jung, Carl, 177
Juvenile delinquency, 129-130, 161

King Phillip's War, 58
Kinsey reports, 64
Klein, Melanie, 175
Krishnamurti, 26
Ku Klux Klan (KKK), 87, 91

Lady Chatterley's Lover, 81-82, 132
Lane, Homer, 26, 104, 106, 129, 185
Lewis, Sinclair, 110
License, defined, 7-8
Lindsay, Judge, 157
Lord of the Flies, 105
Lying:
    by children, 85, 108-112
    by parents, 39-41

Make-up, 143-144
Man Who Knew Coolidge, The, 110
Manners, 27-30, 111
Marriage, 94-97, 154, 156, 159
Masculinity and femininity, 66-67
Masturbation, 64-65, 69, 81, 84, 109, 112, 120, 123
Menstruation, 67
Miller, Henry, 29, 122
Money:
    in adolescence, 147-149
    as substitute for love, 78
Mussolini, Benito, 53

Nudity, 65-66

Obesity, 117
Oedipus reaction, 14, 177

Packard, Vance, 121
Parents:
    attitudes, 169-170
    disagreement between,
        155-161
    family tension, 155-170
    lying to children, 39-41
    personality of, 12, 21-23
Partridge, Eric, 131
Patterson, Floyd, 82
Pavlova, Anna, 39
Peeping Tom, 66
Personality of parent, 12, 21-23
Picasso, Pablo, 51, 177
Plato, 182
Playfair, 184
Plutarch, 182
Politeness, 28. *See also* Manners.
Pornography, 81-82
Property, respect for, 11-12
Psychotherapy, 75, 173-181
    symbolism, 176-178

Reich, 26
Religion, 69, 84-88
Restrictions, on adolescents, 150
Respect:
    for persons, 36-38
    for property, 11-12
    self-respect, 23
Responsibility, 30-35
Robey, George, 52
Royal Air Force (R.A.F.), 89
Russell, Bertrand, 36, 84, 92

Safety, 11, 24
Salk, Jonas, 44

Schools, 45-61. *See also*
    Summerhill School.
    dislike of by children, 45-60
    homework, 60-61
    need for humor, 51-53
    Summerhill principles in
        public schools, 58-60
    teachers, 45-60
Scotland Yard, 51
Scott, Sir Walter, 116
Self-control, defined, 8
Self-government, 26
Self-regulation, 21-26, 106, 151,
    159
Self-respect, 23
Sex, 22, 63-73, 106-107, 127, 128
    circumcision, 67-68
    contraceptives, 68-71
    education, 63-64
    homosexuality, 71-73
    masculinity and femininity,
        66-67
    masturbation, 64-65, 69, 81,
        84, 109, 112, 120, 123
    menstruation, 67
    nudity, 65-66
    Oedipus reaction, 14, 177
    play, 22
Shakespeare, William, 180
Shaw, George Bernard, 19, 48,
    132
Shelley, Percy B., 92
Sibling rivalry, 163-167
Silent Spring, The, 138
Sington, 184
Sleep, 119-121
Smoking, 135-138

Spanking, 99-102, 160-161
Stealing, 112-115
Stekel, Wilhelm, 25, 177-178
Stevenson, Adlai, 52
Strindberg, August, 157
Stuttering, 173
Sulking, 115
Summerhill, 7, 8-9, 21, 76
Summerhill School, 7, 9, 13, 15, 24-25, 26, 29, 30, 33, 42, 51, 53, 56, 57, 58-60, 75, 79, 81, 88, 91, 93, 96, 102, 103, 106, 113, 114, 118, 120, 129, 131, 137, 144, 151, 161, 166, 171, 175, 180, 182, 183
Swearing, 22, 130-134
Symbolism, 176-178

Talks to Parents and Teachers, 185
Tantrums, 23-24
Teachers, 45-60, 176-178
    homework, 60-61
    necessity for sense of humor, 51-53
    using symbolism in classroom, 176-178
    using Summerhill principles in public schools, 58-60
Telephone usage by children, 16

Television, 19-20, 115-116
Tess of the D'Urbervilles, 81
Therapy, 171-182
    dance in, 179-180
    drama in, 182-183
    fear, 171-173
    introversion, 181-182
    psychotherapy, 173-181
    for stuttering, 173
    symbolism, 176-178
Throw Away the Rod, 185
Thumb-sucking, 119
Toilet training, 23
Totentanz, 157
Toys, 121-123
Tropic of Cancer, The, 29, 82, 132

Underprivileged child, 129
Undesirable companions, 83

Vietnam War, 44, 70, 90, 96, 126, 148

Washington, George, 50
When We Dead Awaken, 39
Wilde, Oscar, 8
Wills, David, 185
Work, around the home, 32-35